GOSSIP

Miriam Sagan

Gossip

Tres Chicas Books

ACKNOWLEDGMENTS

Thanks to the following publications in which these essays first appeared.
"Breaking The Rules" first appeared in *Crosswinds* and sections of "Beyond Love
Potion #9" in *The Santa Fe Reporter* and *Magical Blend*. "Credo" is previously
unpublished. All the other essays first appeared in *Sage Magazine*,
sometimes in a somewhat different form and are reprinted
with permission of the *Albuquerque Journal*.

Additional thanks to
Renée Gregorio and Joan Logghe of Tres Chicas Books,
Susannah Sagan, Miriam Bobkoff,
and of course Richard Feldman.

Book design: JB Bryan

Set in Bulmer

Cover photograph: Miriam Bobkoff

ISBN :: 978-1-893003-11-8

Printed on 100% post-consumer waste recycled paper in accordance with
the Green Press Initiative. The mission of the Green Press Initiative is to work
with publishers, industry, and authors to create paper-use transformations
that will conserve natural resources and preserve endangered forests.

Tres Chicas Books
P.O. Box 417
El Rito, New Mexico 87530

Printed in Canada

Contents

Introduction

The personal essay is a time-honored form that focuses on one person's here and now. It begins with the autobiographical impulse to make sense of something general—life or the human condition—in terms of specifics. Paradoxically, the market for literary essays has shrunk in the past decades despite the fact that confession and tell-all dominate the talk shows on the airwaves. But the personal essay of course is not pure confession. Like all essays, it takes a viewpoint and then argues it, even if gently or humorously.

Sage Magazine at *The Albuquerque Journal* has provided a wonderful forum for the personal essay. I've been lucky to have published essays there since its inception, and to have worked with supportive and inspirational editors Polly Summar and Carolyn Flynn. The majority of the essays in this collection first appeared in *Sage*. Over the years, I've been delighted to meet my readers. One essay in particular, "A Spending Diet," provoked a heartfelt response. In it, I wrote about my love of buying socks. As a result, numerous people gave me socks after the essay appeared—and I still get the occasional pair to this day.

Living a life in public isn't always the easiest track. When my husband Rich worked in Albuquerque, he'd often find his coworkers or boss gave him knowing looks on the Monday morning after an essay appeared. As a writer, I've been blessed with a family who hasn't balked much at having the tidbits of their lives used as the rough material for art. For a personal essay is always a dance between the plain truth and the higher one—how the details of life can give meaning to the reader as well as the writer.

Assembling these essays together has been, in some ways, a nostalgic task, like sorting through old photographs. The majority of them were written when I was in my forties, and reflect all the change and flux that decade holds for women. The children who romped through them are grown. Time is a double-edged sword for any writer. Without it, we cannot write, for time itself provides our narrative. And yet to write is to attempt to stop time, at least for a moment. Re-reading and looking back force me to assess what has changed and also what remains the same. What remains is the quality of relationship—with family, friends, the self—something that can be depended upon in many cycles.

Beyond Love Potion Number Nine

I GREW UP IN NEW JERSEY, where women have strong beliefs about love. It was there that I learned the first rule of acquiring a boyfriend: You have to sincerely want one. The girls I grew up with were smart and mean and wore white lipstick. But for all their independence, they wanted, needed, and usually had that essential item—at least one boyfriend. And they did not accept boyfriend substitutes.

Boyfriend substitutes have become far too common among women today. Women suffer under the illusion that they should spend years grieving or processing their last failed relationship. They erroneously think that learning to live alone or having a state-of-the-art sound system is as good as a boyfriend. Such belief systems will keep you single.

Be honest. If you lost your apartment or job, you would not just sit around getting in touch with your feelings or processing the loss. You would take action and start reading the want ads. But first, you have to believe that action is necessary and desirable. So repeat your mantra:

I want a boyfriend
I need a boyfriend
I will *get* a boyfriend.

A few simple steps will help you in your search. It is useful to make a list of every boyfriend you have ever had, and to note how you acquired him. Perhaps you stole him from your roommate or met him at Suds-o-Matic. Get a roommate. Wash the car. What worked once will work again. Place an ad. Implore everyone you know to fix you up. Remember, one woman's ex-husband is another woman's new boyfriend.

Another rule of thumb in looking for a boyfriend is to realize: *you cannot have it all.* The universe will not allow you a boyfriend who fulfills all of your criteria for the perfect man. In fact, the universe will allow you only three conditions, or bottom lines, in the boyfriend search.

Bottom lines are essential, so choose carefully. You may requre a boyfriend who is rich, cute, and well-read ... but you will also have to settle for short and a smoker. In other words, an endless list will get you nowhere. When one friend of mine put in her order for her next husband she said: He must cook, be older than me, like plump women, help with my kids, be part Italian, good at driving in snow and love movies. It did not surprise me when she could not find such a person. Finding your bottom lines is a good predictor for the boyfriend search. Remember, you can't have it all, you don't deserve it all, and you won't get it all.

Still, it is of no use to be overly modest. Bottom lines should not be too pathetic. Your goals for a boyfriend should not look like this:

1. He should not be a pathological liar.
2. He should have a valid driver's license.
3. He should have no felony convictions.

This minimalist approach does not usually result in a boyfriend either.

Figure out your own bottom lines by asking yourself: What can I absolutely not live without? Unfortunately, meeting your bottom lines does not guarantee that your relationship will be a perfect or even an enduring one. But without bottom lines, no relationship stands a chance. They are a bare minimum.

Repeat your mantra: *I want a boyfriend*. Gently mull until you have your three bottom lines. You are now ready for the all important final step: the boyfriend ritual.

Love rituals and potions are nothing new. In fact, ever since Eve offered Adam that apple, women have been dabbling in a bit of kitchen magic, concocting something that will draw or keep or get rid of love. I was initiated into these ancient mysteries quite by accident many years ago, when I lived in a big communal house in San Francisco. One of my male roommates had just broken up with his girlfriend, who had actually left him because she was now blissfully, passionately, in love with her boss—a woman. The ex-girlfriend called him about returning some books and clothes, but I answered the phone. "Miriam," she whispered excitedly. "I've discovered this fantastic love ritual. Do it, and you'll fall in love. Take a candle, write on it three times with a rose thorn 'All My Loves Come to Me' and burn it down. It works. You have to try it!" I was quite dubious, but she insisted it would work. "The only problem is," she added in a warning tone, "is that sometimes it just draws raw lust first. You have to be careful to distinguish between love and lust."

Of course I couldn't resist tryng this love ritual. I didn't have a handy rose thorn, so I used a Bic pen instead. In a matter of weeks, all of my old sweeties had appeared back on the scene and were chasing me madly. This must have been the lust part. But sure enough, in a few months I was in love, and a year later I was married.

Over the years, I've heard about other love rituals. The candle seems to be the most powerful, but others might be worth tryimg. I have a friend in L.A. who swears by the ritual of placing a personal ad. When she has wanted to get into a new relationship, she writes up the ad, clearly visualizing what she wants in a mate. When the responses pour in, she looks them over, but never seems to have time to answer them, because the ad works as a kind of charm. The first time she placed an ad she went out on a blind date set up by friends which turned into a long term relationship. The second time, she was asked out by an old friend she ended up marrying. So for this woman, the personal ad is a way of telling herself and the universe she is ready for love. And for many women, love rituals can be about redefining personal space. Some buy new sheets at the start of a relationship, some smudge a room to get rid of an old lover's "vibes." Many a woman has changed the position of her bed to change the inclinations of her heart. Housecleaning itself can be a kind of love magic.

My friend Shura, a romantic world traveller, took a dim view of her own love life after she became the single mother of a young son. But for her, her bed, and not housecleaning, was the central focal point of her ritual. She placed a bowl of salt beneath her bed, just under where her heart would be when she was sleeping. She left it there for ten days, then took it out and burned the salt, not on a witches' bonfire but in a pan on her own stove. Three months later, she had a boyfriend who wanted to marry her and adopt her son. Becoming more cautious in matters of love, she said she'd need some time to decide. But she was convinced that the ritual, which she'd found printed in an ordinary newspaper in Spain, had worked overtime!

Some women take a cautious view of love magic. My friend Ana went on vacation to Oaxaca. She came back with a collection of magical amulets and little pocket pillows, all charms for love. She opened a heart-shaped box to reveal a tiny red hand-stitched satin pillow adorned with a picture of a man and woman embracing. Another showed lovers in a clinch beneath a hummingbird and a pair of disembodied hands throwing wedding rice or love powder. A pink one was adorned with a flower and the words "Flor de Sandalo: para regos purificantes." But although these looked as innocuous as cosmetics, Ana wouldn't use them. "You never know what it's going to do," she said of a love charm. "Until I know how to put parameters on it, I'm not doing anything." She suggested creating a love nicho, rather than using powder, because a nicho is contained and you can close the doors. To create a love nicho, she advisesd starting with protection or defense, so the energy does not get out of hand. She'd use a protective incantation, such as "let nothing low or dark enter here." In the nicho itself, place something red, and then something which belongs to the love object, such as a button.

As a teenager in New Jersey, I believed in the superstition that green M & M's were aphrodisiacs. I currently favor the ancient Jewish belief that giving charity in denominations of 18, the number that symbolizes life, can draw your true mate to you. It may be that the greatest love charm is love itself—yearning, need, desire. Send it out, and see what you get back.

How to Flirt

"FLIRTING IS ATTENTION WITHOUT INTENTION," says my sister Susannah. I don't know if she's quoting Jane Austen, Bette Davis, or herself, but she's right. Flirting is an essentially innocent activity, and it's easier to do if you feel it doesn't really imply very much. Its virtue is that it can add spice to even the most mundane situation. Flirting is one of life's true pleasures, but many of the women I know are afraid of it. They are worried they don't know how to do it, that they are too serious for such frivolity, or just plain too shy. Not so those in my family; we inherited the skill from my mother, a serious flirt. Now even after fifty years of marriage, she is still practicing the art. "It's you!" she'll exclaim with enthusiasm when my father walks into the room as if he had been gone five years rather than five minutes. Flirting can be learned, and all it takes is a little practice.

It's best to learn the basics of flirting on something that cannot be considered a serious potential love object. You can even practice on a potted plant, or a cat, but babies are far and away the best. In fact, babies can be considered the origin of flirting. Consider the game of peek-a-boo. All it takes to make a baby smile or even giggle is the simple trick of looking directly at the baby, then looking away. If you stare too long at a baby, the baby is apt to get overwhelmed, and maybe even start wailing. So keep it light. Add the classic gesture of covering your eyes with your hands, and the baby will adore you.

Practicing on a baby will win you friends—the baby and baby's doting relatives. It will also free you up from the misguided notion that flirting is somehow attention with intention. You need not flirt for the purpose of getting a date, true love, or a long-term commitment. Flirting is its own reward as an enjoyable activity. Since the baby is safe to flirt with, you may as well practice on babies until you feel more confident.

A friend of mine recently exited a long-term relationship complaining that she couldn't flirt. She felt faintly unattractive and generally just out of shape as far as the opposite sex was concerned. Flirting is the aerobics of relationships, however. Flirting, by its very nature, puts you back into shape. The first thing my friend needed to remember was that flirting didn't necessary indicate any real interest or availability on her part. It was a safe exercise, but one which might also stretch long dormant muscles.

"With those big brown eyes," I told her, "you should have no trouble at all."

"But what should I do?"

"Just remember the basics: look, then look away."

"That's all?"

"Yup. And your assignment is to do it three times, just with anybody or anything . . . "

My friend called the next day. "I took your assignment," she said. "I just went ahead and flirted with this very elderly safe looking guy in a truck . . . look, look away . . . and he smiled at me. Then, just a few hours later, this old friend called and confessed he had always had a crush on me, and now that I was available . . . "

This of course is an unusual success story. Two minutes of flirting will not normally lead to instant true love. But in some mysterious way, flirting creates positive energy around you and that can lead to just about anything.

Sticking with family tradition, I wanted to impress upon my daughter Isabel the importance of flirting. When she was twelve years old, I came upon her and a friend looking at themselves in the mirror. They were embellishing their cheekbones with glitter gloss and brushing their hair till it was beyond shiny.

"What are you doing?" I was curious.

"We want to get boys to look at us."

"That isn't how to get boys to look at you," I said.

"Why not?"

"Boys are afraid of you," I said, remembering seventh grade and maybe many years beyond. "You have to flirt."

"How?"

"Look down," I instructed. They did.

"Now look up . . . "

They looked up.

"Now say 'hi'."

"Hi," they chorused.

"Just practice," I said.

I don't think my daughter will ever credit this technique, but she did not lack for middle school boyfriends. And the discussion reminded me of one of the essentials of flirting—other people are shy and afraid too. Your potential love object is just as nervous as you are. Flirting is reassuring, even relaxing.

Flirting is not just to attract strangers. One of the greatest uses of flirting is to keep a permanent relationship juicy. Why flirt, you might think, I've already got this guy! But remember, flirting is attention without intention, and everyone loves attention. Also, I believe it's good to stay in practice as a flirt. Based on all this, I frequently practice flirting with my husband Rich. I tease him, I compliment him, and then I ignore him. (This is just an expansion of the look—look away technique). Pretty soon, he's paying a lot of attention to me as well.

The only problem is, he knows I like to flirt on principle. "Are you bored?" he asks. "Are you flirting with me just because you have nothing better to do? Shall I lend you a good book to read?"

"No," I say, "I'd rather be with you."

Now, that is flirting.

Breaking the Rules

RELATIONSHIPS BETWEEN THE SEXES are endlessly perplexing, which is why we rush out to read books which purport to finally explain *The Rules,* why *Men Are from Mars* or why we are *Women Who Love Too Much.* The book *The Rules* —by Ellen Fein and Sherrie Schneider—was a bestseller some years ago. Now it is perhaps passé—supplanted by whatever is the newest in the "how to catch a man" genre. But almost every woman has heard of *The Rules* if not actually read them. *The Rules* have been parodied, attacked, and yes, slavishly followed. Of course, the rules are nothing new, but basically a 1950's-esque formula for how to get a man to marry you. Your grandmother would approve. But can we?

Let's leave aside for the moment the question of whether or not a husband is even worth pursuing. Maybe you are content with your cat, or have three lovers, prefer a hermit's cabin or playing the field. The question is, do these kind of rules provide any kind of road map to relationships between the sexes here at the start of the new millennium?

To begin with, the rules will only work if you subscribe to at least a mildly combative view of love. This is indeed the traditional view, for as the Latin poet Ovid wrote in his "Art of Love": "Love is a kind of war/And no assignment for cowards." The Middle Ages in Europe brought primers of courtly love which instructed a callow knight on how to woo and win his lady. And the twentieth century brought us more self-help books and how-to articles on the subject than could be read by any one woman in her lifetime.

But the women's movement supposedly changed the rules of love. Now women and men were equal partners, and women everywhere were gleefully breaking grandma's injunctions to never pick up the check or ask a man out on a date.

But apparently women still aren't happy with men, if the rate at which self-help books are selling is any indication. *The Rules* counsels *never* appearing to be too available to a potential mate. Rules Girls, as they call themselves, don't look too eager, always get off the phone first, never accept a date on short notice, and don't live with a man they aren't engaged to. Rules Girls are also instructed—in almost cult-like fashion—to never—never!—break these rules, and to never discuss the program with their therapists.

However, I have followed a different set of rules since I was thirteen years old—and in the main have been happy in love. This set of rules is indigenous to the place I was raised, but you don't need to have been born in New Jersey to follow The Jersey Girl Rules.

In New Jersey when I was growing up, the war between the sexes often seemed to reach rumble proportions. Boys and then men were obscure, unpredictable creatures who could ruin your equanimity in a nanosecond. To navigate the minefield of relationships, my friends and I devised and lived by a particular code. I came of age in New Jersey in a subculture of girls out to catch boys. It had its own earthy if primitive rules that applied to the war between the sexes.

The main rule was that girls were basically irresistible to boys, and that if you gave a guy a soulful enough French kiss he would be your slave. The girls I grew up with, however, did scorn the idea that they could be slaves to boys. The only girl in our clique who was reputed to have served her boyfriend breakfast in bed while she wore only an apron was roundly laughed at. Total Womanhood, Marabel Morgan style, was out. Sex and mystery, Anais Nin style, was in.

The Rules is a bit more sophisticated than a bunch of Jersey girls, but not necessarily more convincing. *The Rules* sold because the theory mixes some real truth with some serious lies. The authors do have a few good points, the best being that a woman can't make a man love her who doesn't naturally. And the corollary is good too: if he doesn't love you, get rid of him. Another positive injunction from *The Rules* is that a woman should develop her own life and interests, and not just sit around waiting for a man to call.

When the book was at its zenith, I did a bit of primary research. Although I first maligned the book for being antifeminist, I then tried the rules. Since my significant other was already living in my house, I just practiced being busy, and hopefully mysterious. I picked up a large book every time he came into the room, I stopped calling him at work. "I feel as if I haven't seen you in days," he complained. Okay, so I had his attention and I'd gotten some reading done. But I usually had his attention, now he just seemed confused by my lack of interest. It didn't seem worth the manipulation.

Still, as a Jersey Girl, I do naturally follow some of the rules. For example. I never cruise parties for men (a rules no-no) because I actually enjoy talking to people regardless of age or gender. "But not every woman knows not to give herself away," says one of my Rules Girlfriends. "We have to follow the rules. We need to learn." And my grapevine tells me that there are ladies about town with rules support groups, and some who carry copies of the main rules with them to consult on powder breaks during dates.

Of course, critics point out the main flaw in *The Rules*: no one, not even the most determined woman, can keep up a sham forever. The rules won't work too well in an actual intimate relationship, anymore than prancing around in a negligee will. The best bet, of course, is to make your own rules. The genie in Disney's "Aladdin" hisses in the courting hero's ear: "Be yourself!" Maybe be your best self—your most independent and charming self, but the rules don't let you discover your own romantic persona which are as variable as the human soul. Only you can determine what mixture of mystery and honesty work best for who you are.

However, if you need some help, here are the Jersey Girl Rules to give you some guidance.

The Jersey Girl Rules

1. Men are naturally your slaves. This is the most important rule, and the one that is the most difficult to remember. However, think about history, the

Trojan War fought for Helen of Troy. Think of literature, Romeo killing himself over Juliet. Think of contemporary statistics, where unmarried men die younger than married men (unmarried women do just fine!). Try not to question this dictum, or look critically in the mirror and say "well, men certainly are not *my* slaves." This is not something you have to live up to. Accept it as true, even if you have to fake belief at first.

2. A. Men are not women. This would seem obvious, but it is a rule we are constantly tempted to violate. Whether the man in question is a boyfriend, husband, friend, or date, never under any circumstances discuss anything remotely to do with female biology with him—whether childbirth or pantyhose. Feminine mystery is instantly violated by words like "yeast infection." You have friends. Talk to them instead.

2. B. You must never ask a man if you look fat. This is a corollary of rule 2. A. My sister Rachel once said: "Any man can be trained to eventually say 'yes, you do look like you've gained a little weight.'" And these are words you do not want to hear. It is of course possible that if you live with a man for a long time you will occasionally break this rule. In which case, do what I do, run shrieking from the room exclaiming "I can't believe I broke Jersey Girl Rule 2.B.!" This should make him forget the fat question.

3. Indifference only works if you want to stay single. Needy women, rude women, women in pastel pantsuits all have husbands. Obviously one is not rewarded for virtue or chic when it comes to men. This is the rule that took me the longest to understand. I kept thinking I had to be adorable and charming to attract men. But if you'll refer back to Rule 1, you will see this isn't necessary. Acting like you want a guy is the way to signal to him that you want him—nothing more or less. I know that your mother and *The Rules* tell you not to do this, but the author of *The Rules* is divorced, and I bet your mother isn't playing hard to get with your father.

4. Jealousy is your friend. I know this goes against all the advice you'll ever find in a self-help book, because jealousy has gone out of fashion. And no doubt it is best to avoid the psycho-jealousy that can land you in court on a felony rap. But garden variety jealousy is a great aid to love. If someone else is flirting with your sweetie, move in and stake your turf. Make it clear to your guy that you consider him yours and yours alone.

5. You don't have to be from New Jersey to profit from the Jersey Girl Rules. In fact, you can use them even if you've never even been to the Garden State. I've known Jersey Girls from Taos and Brooklyn, San Francisco and Boston. And they've all been, if not perfectly happy in their lives, successful in love.

The Return of the Boyfriend

My HIGH SCHOOL BOYFRIEND was a skinny handsome guy who looked romantically pale beneath a grungy beard and lack of haircut. He wore a beat up old jacket that might wash out to navy blue. My mother despaired of him, often saying "I think Richard would look so nice in some classic clothes!" His only classic was a black beret, reminiscent of Che Guevara.

As we said in those days, "we became boyfriend and girlfriend" when I was fifteen and he was sixteen. I was the first girl he ever kissed. We had a lot in common, were from similar backgrounds, cared about school, liked to gossip and chat, and go out exploring. It was a "serious" relationship. My parents, no doubt thinking a graduate school-bound boyfriend a better vice than the other temptations of the early 1970's, did not disown me when we lived together the summer before I went to college. Liberal as they were, though, they did swear me to secrecy—I was not to tell my younger siblings for fear of being a bad influence. But Richard and I thought we'd get married, be together always.

That summer of playing house was a bit premature for me, though. I was glad to hit the dorm in the fall—a co-ed dorm at that. Boys seemed to be everywhere, and I went boy crazy. By winter, I broke up with my high school love Richard—precipitously, rudely. I wanted to be free, as we said in those days. And there were things about Rich that just weren't perfect—he was a terrible dresser, known for matching paisley and stripes. He was a little too serious, perhaps, a bit too responsible. And he had never told me he loved me. Never. Despite the passion between, he was disconcertingly mute.

So I was free. I met a man who told me he loved me six times a day, then broke my heart. I moved to San Francisco, and married a skinny, handsome man, Robert, with whom I also had a lot in common. He had his faults too—a bad temper, which I confused with a passionate nature, and a disinterest in making a living, which I thought the sign of a free spirit. Still, we liked to chat, gossip, and go out exploring. My husband was kind-hearted and emotionally dependable, and yes, he told me he loved me.

Richard and I were in touch over those years—by phone, letter, an occasional visit. I apologized for the way I broke up with him. Oddly, he'd ended up "being free" in a more extreme way than I had—hitchhiking twice across the country and living for a decade in communes. We thanked each other belatedly for our mutual initiation, when as adults we found that most peoples' stories were not as sweet and gentle-hearted as ours. Richard still seemed cute and skinny to me, a terrible dresser, perhaps a bit too serious.

Then, an unforeseen life drama struck. I was widowed at the age of forty-one. My daughter was six. Robert had been a mere thirty-six, and died from unexpected complications from surgery. In the weeks after the death, I was seized with a desire to talk to Richard. I couldn't explain it, but it was partially that my husband's death made me feel as if my past had been wiped away. It was terrifying. My old friends were suddenly very special. I wanted to see the boyfriend who had known me when.

Perhaps it was more than that. When he got off the plane, my heart was pounding, my mouth dry. He looked skinny and handsome and was well-dressed in a pink shirt and tie since he had now joined the professional world. And he was still wearing a black beret. But he was much too serious. As we talked, I kept thinking: not for me. Perhaps I was protesting too much, but we were certainly in very different states. I had just experienced death and traumatic loss, which made me reckless. Richard had been without a love interest for four long years, which made him more cautious. He told me seriously that he wasn't looking for anything casual ever again, he wanted to get married for the first time, settle down.

We spent a pleasant day together. Pleasant, just pleasant. From this I concluded that he was no longer attracted to me—that I was too old, too fat, and much too morose. It didn't occur to me that it might be gentlemanly not to jump on the recently widowed. Richard just seemed too cautious, without a daring cell in his body.

Then we fell into the clinch. After all, it was like old times . . . I was the first woman he'd kissed in four years. When the visit ended, we promised to meet again. And so after some visiting and back and forth discussion we spent the summer together just miles from where we'd first kept house in Boston. Only this time I was visiting from New Mexico, and I had a daughter and Richard had a closetful of suits. My daughter seemed at home with Rich. She'd told me to marry him the first time he'd visited, but I hadn't paid much attention, knowing the children of widows often tried to fix their moms up with anyone and everyone. Still, the bond between them grew. He taught her to play chess, to cook eggs. She taught him to play Candyland, and to build a fort of furniture. She was clear, with a child's honesty, that he wasn't her Dad, who she would always miss. But I could feel her relax and grow, with two adults to parent her. It felt so right for all of us, and I discovered that Richard's and my earlier relationship had formed a lifelong paradigm for me of intimacy: I was never happier than listening to music over dinner, reading a funny tidbit out loud, planning a trip.

I couldn't very well accuse Richard of not being daring when he threw up job and apartment that fall to move into my house two thousand miles away from all that was familiar. This time it was easier to tell my sisters and brother than my parents. What would my folks think about suddenly being related to a boyfriend they'd considered long gone? To my surprise, my mother and father were wholeheartedly delighted. In general, I noticed that friends and relatives of the previous generation were completely supportive. As a widow, I had the most understanding from older folks who had experienced death and loss, and who knew that happiness can be a rare chance. Richard's parents greeted me and my daughter with open arms. In fact, the biggest problem anyone seemed to have was what to wear to the wedding.

And so we got engaged, married, lived happily ever after. What changed in my appraisal of this man in the intervening twenty five years? For one thing, I learned that everyone has faults, even, to my surprise, me. Thirteen years of marriage had also taught me a lifetime's lessons about the play between intimacy and boundaries. I no longer imagined, as I did in high school, that there was a perfect love out there that would complete me. Richard had changed too. For one thing, he had learned to say: I love you. But a lot about him hadn't changed. I'd just grown to like a steady dependable man, and to value consistency. Besides, as my mother had predicted, he looked great in a tie and pink Oxford shirt.

Marriage—Is It Back?

Around the time that Richard and I were married, by seeming coincidence, we were invited to a run of weddings. It was at a wedding shower for a second-time bride that I observed the following. Despite the usual ooh and aah-ing over lacey underwear and scented bath oil, there was something else at the gathering—cynicism. It wasn't directed at the bride, obviously in love and making a compatible match, or even at the rituals of marriage. Rather, it was a cynicism directed at man-woman relationships. The woman next to me sipped some champagne and speared a shrimp. "Sometimes," she sighed, "I don't even know why we try."

Certainly a generation ago wedding showers were as not full of tales of divorce and the attendant pessimism. And yet, marriage is still in, with a rate the highest it has been in decades. Since my first marriage ended when I was widowed, I probably have a less cynical view than if I were divorced. Still, in the past year, I had been to four other weddings, and all of the couples were in their late thirties or over forty. Of this group, five of the eight people involved had never been married before. Among my peers, weddings were rampant.

Marriage remains a problematic—never unambivalent—thing for women of the baby boomer generation. I found that my announcement of impending matrimony was greeted by my friends a with eighty percent wild enthusiasm and twenty percent cynical horror. My peers, it seems, don't view the prospect of marriage as an unconflicted good the way a Jane Austen heroine would, or even my own mother.

"I hope you're not doing this just to not be alone," a self-sufficient friend chided. I couldn't help snapping back: "Well, that worked alright the first time." I was being facetious of course, and over the thirteen year course of a mostly happy first marriage I learned that marriage certainly is no antidote to loneliness. Lack of communication can hurt much more than physically being alone. But I'd also learned to enjoy just plain old company—sharing a day, plans, jokes.

"It's just that marriage is SO . . . scary!" a never-married friend told me, widening her catlike green eyes. I didn't point out that she'd done plenty of scary things—from mountain climbing to complicated romances—because basically I agreed with her. Marriage is scary, but not perhaps for the obvious reasons. Both men and women say they're afraid of commitment, but having children or a career or even a garden takes just that. I think what we're really afraid of is intimacy—the sense that another human being can see you, want things from you, disappoint you, and yes, still be there the next morning or month or year.

A recently divorced friend told me that friends encouraged her to go it alone. Somehow, her women friends implied, a truly strong person doesn't need anyone else. Self-sufficiency is the American way, and its almost a cultural truism that the highest state is to be in a nation of one. This may come in part from looking at traditional marriage and seeing the confines of our foremothers' lives, or suffering through relationships that can easily bear the nasty labels of the moment: codepenent or dysfunctional. My divorced friend spent a year on her own, in part just to see if she could do it. Then she got involved with a new man. "It's harder," she says "to be involved with somebody. You have to be awake. But it's worth it."

What surprised me is that women don't think being involved with a man is fun. I can't make a universal theory out of this, but I wouldn't have gotten married again if I didn't enjoy the heck out of it. I like the sense of the unpredictable, the fresh perspective, that someone else brings to my household. I like being teased about my habits, and being brought soup when I'm sick.

Certainly one in two marriages ends in divorce. And marriage is an optimistic occupation, if not an entirely rational one. Of course it's good that my friends don't feel they have to be married to live fulfilling lives. Still, I'm glad my friends gave me a bachelorette party instead of just critiquing the institution. A twice-married friend, who has both an ironic and a sentimental side, said it best for me. "We come into this world alone," she said, "and our job is to learn how to get on with SOMEBODY. What better way than marriage?"

Middle-Aged Love

Of all the weddings that Rich and I attended, one was particularly charming. The summer rain stopped just in time for the ceremony to be held under a massive cottonwood. The bride looked beautiful, the groom handsome, the parents proud, the guests celebratory. After plenty of food and drink, the guests began to dance and toast. But walking hand-in-hand in the moonlight across little bridges over reflecting pools were several couples who looked happier than anyone else at the party. All of these couples were well past their youth, all of them were at least second-time-around (or more!) marriages or long-term relationships. And yet they seemed as enraptured, or more, with each other's company than younger couples. What was going on?

Our image of romance in this society is heavily based on youth. After all, Romeo and Juliet were dead in each others' arms at an age when we haven't even graduated from high school. Youth seems to be it for beauty and passion. But when we look around at our friends and acquaintances, not to mention ourselves, most of us just aren't with those we loved when we were callow. And many of us are on our second, or even third, marriage or committed relationship. The myth goes, particularly for women, that by the time we reach a "certain age" and have a bit of sag and bulge, not to mention experience of life, we are essentially washed up and beyond romance. Yet I have numerous friends who at forty or fifty or sixty—and yes, even older—seem to be embarking on the happiest love relationships of their lives.

"You learn that infatuation isn't everything, lust isn't everything," one of the middle-aged wedding guests said, leaning back over coffee. I was a little surprised by his statement, because I knew his relationship was a passionate one. "It isn't everything," he clarified, "other things are more important, like companionship." These words would have traumatized me when I was younger. When I was in my twenties, passion was everything, preferably a blind infatuation with some fellow who on closer inspection might prove to just be a standard issue bad boyfriend—thoughtless, self-engrossed, and domineering.

Companionship may be a dirty word to the young, but to my older ears it sounds a lot like friendship. Friendship was certainly touted in bygone times as one of the pinnacles of human relationships—compassionate, caring, selfless—but it has fallen into disrepair in ours. We don't seem to have the time or inclination for true friendship much any more, because friendship is low-key and needs sustaining. But friendship does play a great part in love. We want the best for our friends—and we let them define what that might be. In contrast, we want our love objects to meet our needs, surely a more selfish way to deal with another. But one thing I have noticed about love later in life—there is more acceptance, and less of trying to make the other person over. Maybe it's because we actually realize such effort is doomed to failure. As older partners, we come to each other with complete histories—not to mention ex-spouses, mortgages, alimony, and teen-aged or adult children. We have to accept each other—what you see is what you get, and there is less illusion. But this isn't a bad thing at all.

I've heard my father muse on the relationships he has seen around him that started in middle age. "People seem to have fun," he says contemplatively, "they just seem to get on with each other." Fun may be something we associate with dating, but not necessarily with building a life together. Buying a house, raising children, advancing professionally—these things may be worthwhile but they can hardly be generally characterized as fun. For somewhat older couples, some of these struggles are in the past—we succeeded, or failed, our expectations have changed, and in some new lease on the life force we seem ready for fun again. When I see such men and women wrapped up together in a love of travel or pottery or theater or gardening, I know they are having fun.

Sometimes when I see a very old couple who have been married almost their whole lives, I'm awash in envy. Here are those who chose each other, and weren't prematurely separated by death or divorce. In fact, I'd venture to say that for almost any couple, time has the mellowing effect of love the second time around. But walking in the moonlight with my (yes, second) husband, I couldn't have been happier on that summer night at the wedding. Observing middle-aged love has given me trust in how life and love go on, and even can get better with time.

What Guys Want

IT IS MY OBSERVATION that women spend countless and often fruitless hours trying to figure out what men want. The dark side of this is that as women we secretly want men to need and desire certain things on our agendas rather than listening to them. So I decided to ask the men in my life. My brother Daniel—a man in his forties with two kids—paused and looked thoughtfully into the air in front of him. His life was often hectic—he ran a business, taught architecture, and did his share of cooking, cleaning, and childcare. He mused for a moment and then said: "Men want to be occasionally bathed in the warm bath of approval." I could extrapolate that men have a basic need—to be appreciated for who they are.

A few years ago a book came out that was a topic of family discussion. A woman in Berkeley placed a personal ad before her seventieth birthday. The gist was that she'd never known true passion—and was looking for the man who could provide it. Much to our surprise she got many responses and wrote a book about her experiences—belying the truism that no one thinks elderly ladies are sexy. Why did her ad work? My father waxed philosophic. "Guys want to feel needed. They want to be helpful. And here was this lady asking for help with sex!" But then he cautioned—"and men like to feel a woman needs their help. The trouble starts when they discover she is also self-sufficient . . . "

Then I asked my husband—potentially a more volatile answerer than my father or brother. What if he said men want an eternally gorgeous, young, and pliable woman or something else I could never be? But my husband's view wasn't that different from my brother's, although perhaps tempered a bit by years. He said "Women want men to change but men want to be loved for themselves." I then concluded my research by asking a male friend what men were looking for in a woman to date and mate. He said that the women who were the most successful with men where those who genuinely liked the male species—and (once again) weren't about to change them.

Sigmund Freud asked famously, and perhaps with some personal frustration: "What do women want?" As women, we could probably rush right in and tell him—respect, appreciation, freedom to make our own decisions, trust in our judgment. Not too suprisingly, this is what men want too. But often the women in their lives run roughshod over this need. You may think that throwing out his old shirt or criticizing the way he cares for the kids is just being helpful—but there probably isn't a woman alive who wouldn't rebel at being on the receiving end of such treatment. The advice to accept and approve falls on our collectively deaf ears. Many women, secretly or overtly, regard their partners and even their casual dates as fixer-upper projects, rather like a run-down property that shows promise and needs work. In fact, we may even confuse this attitude with love itself. After all, we show our appreciation of everything from our houses to our babies by picking up, rectifying, improving, coaching, etc. The dark heart of this attitude emerges in the talk of many women who casually say: "Oh, all men are babies." This attitude, of superiority mixed with perhaps disappointment, is one that would shock and outrage us if it were directed at the female half of the human race.

But what about the idea that women are from Venus and men from some planet that can't commit? Be careful about generalizing from a temporary stage in a man's life. Sure, a man may be in a state where he wants to play the field and flees from feminine attempts to entrap him. But many a woman has been startled to lose a roamer only to find him happily married to some other woman a few months later. It may simply be that she wasn't the right woman in his opinion—or that he simply wasn't in a settling mood. When men decide to commit they often move fast, feeling "it's time." And it is usually impossible to try and convince a guy that you're the one or that this is the time (and don't forget, it might be difficult to convince *you* of this as well).

To bathe a man in a warm bath of approval you may have to give up certain deeply held, but stereotyped, notions of his behavior. He is not a baby. Use your good judgment to ascertain if he is a playboy, addict, or man with serious problems. Screening these out, your practice is indeed to treat him as you yourself would like to be treated. Some of these old-fashioned virtues—respect, helpfulness, compassion—aren't highlighted as much in today's world of glitz and fast fixes. But since acceptance is what men say they want—and as acceptance is a positive value for the giver as well as the receiver—we might stop trying to change them. And enjoy them instead.

Dinner with Mr. X

TWENTY-FIVE YEARS AFTER my old boyfriend walked out on me, he showed up in town on business and asked to take me to dinner. Of course I had mixed feelings about this. He was a man I had adored—and the only serious relationship I'd ever had in which I'd been dumped. On the other hand, I'd been married twice since then, and was currently very happy. So I said yes. Of course there was the usual neurosis about seeing an old boyfriend. I soon gave up on the idea that I could lose twenty pounds in five days and decided to concentrate on my outfit. My old friend Carol, who knew me well—both then and now—gave me a strict lecture. "Do not," she instructed "wear one of your Hawaiian shirts covered in tropical flowers just to show you don't care. Dress up! Look good! The honor of womankind is at stake!" She was my only friend who had even known me back when I adored Mr. X. She empathized with my mix of panic and curiosity, and said I could call her on my cell from the women's room if I needed on-the-scene advice. Bolstered by her support, I looked at my wardrobe.

I settled on a nice black chiffon dress and a nice strand of black pearls. I wanted to look like what I was—safely married. I picked a restaurant I liked, and yes, an expensive one. I arrived a bit early to give myself the observer's advantage—I'd see him first. Waiting outside the restaurant in the balmy evening air I saw Mr. X saunter in from across the street. He looked exactly the same—boyish and handsome. He had changed shockingly little. He looked like trouble.

"I'm going to write an article about having dinner with you," I announced as soon as we were seated. I wanted to put him on guard.

He responded in kind, parodying a romance novel, "As soon as I saw him, the unmistakable power of his masculinity overcame me."

"Uh uh," I said, "When I saw him enter the restaurant I knew he hadn't changed at all—and that wasn't good," I retorted.

Mr. X had also asked to come back and meet my family after dinner, but I was wary. So I began a rating system. If he got a high score, I might let him. He flirted with the waitress—points off. He had pictures of his kids—add points. He leered when I nervously dropped mashed potatoes down my shirt—points off. He spoke highly of his wife—add points.

However, the general impression that I got from Mr. X was that he was a nice guy—just not the guy for me. How could I have been so deluded when I thought I wanted to spend the rest of my life with him? He was a high energy guy who thrived on combat, both professionally and personally. I liked the quiet life. He lived in the east—I in the west. There were some areas of compatibility, though. We were both devoted to our families, we both cared about social justice and about art. But experience had taught me what youthful passion could not—a couple needs to be compatible in the details of daily living or at least complementary. When we were young, Mr. X's idea of a weekend morning was to bolt up at dawn and go the hardware store in search of home improvement. Mine was to sleep in. He thought me slothful; I considered him hyper. Mr. X liked parties, I liked to read. Mr. X wanted the house to look furnished in a certain style, I could have cared less. Our compatibility factors sometimes crossed but never truly intersected.

When Mr. X left me, I was distraught. I felt my life was over, and that I would never love again. I lay on the floor of my lonely, now underfurnished, apartment and sobbed for what felt like months. My sister Rachel, however, had something very pointed to say. "You loved Mr. X for the wrong reasons," she said. "You basically loved him because you thought he was gorgeous and sexy and wild. He loved you for the right reasons—because you were smart and warm—but he knew that wasn't enough. He was right to leave. He did you a favor."

Maybe he did. Once I stopped sobbing, I moved to California and completely changed my life. Now in this one, Mr. X chivalrously picked up the bill. I decided to invite him back. He was greeted by my daughter, who showed a sudden and unusual interest in adults—of course she had heard me talk about him. My husband Rich also seemed charged with an alertness brought on by the proximity of his wife's old boyfriend—he became unusually witty and charming. In fact, he made a pun in French, a language he hadn't studied since high school, as if suddenly multi-lingual and ultra-debonaire.

Mr. X sat down at our kitchen table and proceeded to do magic tricks. He made the sugar in the sugar bowl disappear and then reappear up his sleeve. My daughter and husband laughed—they were charmed. I, however, couldn't help but think there was a metaphor here. There had been several illusions at play. Just because Mr. X was cute, I had thought he was also the one for me. In addition, Mr. X had changed from my bad ex-boyfriend into someone else's perfectly good husband. In a way, this dinner had also been a kind of magic trick. He had changed from Mr. Bad Who Left Me into simply Mr. Not Quite The Right One.

Gossip

GOSSIP—MY RELIGION FORBIDS IT and probably yours does too. Gossip—I've spent my whole life listening to it, adding to it, and passing it on. Gossip—it shares a root with the word gospel, which means truth. So what is the truth about gossip?

Gossip can be loosely defined as talking about someone behind her or his back, an activity at which my large extended circle of acquaintance excels. There are really two categories of gossip: 1. simply talking about someone in a way you never would if that someone were present (Did you see that hat? And no one that old should be at a wedding in that dress) and 2. information which is ostensibly a secret and yet that is being passed around at a great rate.

So, is gossiping bad for you? I'll look at the positive—or gospel—side first. If it weren't for novels, movies, and gossip, I'd know a lot less about human nature than I do. Gossip in high school taught me a lot about the opposite sex—and our success and failure with them. It taught me what to wear, and what to not wear. It taught me about how appearance is perceived and what other people are thinking.

On the negative side, gossip in high school, and beyond, taught me to feel that other peoples' problems needed my opinion: she did what!? He ran around on her but then she . . . only a complete bimbo etc. would . . . Gossip is critical and it creates a separation. We who are gossiping feel morally superior to the subject in question—we haven't run up credit card debt, dated a Lothario, cheated on our mate, lost our looks, (fill in your favorite bit of gossip here). Gossip is a paradox—on the one hand it gives me a sense that I'm not alone in my human foibles, but on the other hand it does just the opposite—it makes me feel superior and critical. And so, I've tried to develop a few policies about gossip. I can't always stick to them, but at least they create a trend.

Sometimes gossip can express a sense of missed connection. Let us say I'm talking to one of my friends about another friend—she never calls, or she calls and never asks how I am, she draws me into drama and never tells me when things resolve, she forgot my birthday, and the litany goes on. This may be letting off steam, but it is essentially just bad-mouthing. So my first gossip reform was to realize that I had to stop this and speak directly to the person who was bothering me. My current gossip policy is to allow myself a few complaints and then address the problem directly.

But what about secrets? Secret gossip has too often been my downfall. Recently a casual friend said: "I have something incredibly juicy—horrible actually—to tell you, but you must swear to secrecy!" Now, years ago I realized that I just wasn't designed to feel happy keeping secrets. I once kept a very destructive secret for years at some cost. My relief when the truth came out was so great that I realized I just had to say no to secrets. But even the best intentions fail. I wanted to hear something juicy and horrible. I said yes, I heard the gossipy secret, and immediately felt bad. Then, before I knew it, my lip was unbuttoned and I was gossiping to a third party about this secret. It made me feel uncomfortable, it worried me, I just had to share it—but these rationalizations didn't make me feel any better.

I ended up consulting with a therapist who gave me some good common sense advice I could have given myself if I'd been clear. The therapist told me to go back to the original friend and tell her I couldn't keep the secret. I was very worried about this, but when I did she was receptive. I said I wasn't planning to broadcast to the world, but I just couldn't be under an oath of silence. Luckily, she understood, and I've resolved more than ever to keep no toxic secrets.

However, the flip of that is discretion. Without pressure to be secretive, I want to gossip less. When a friend asks how a mutual friend is I want to say "Fine, and I know she'd love to hear from you," rather than giving my opinion on said friend's hair, children, and relationships. I've improved even in writing this essay. Writers suffer particularly from a compulsion to gossip—although we may call it storytelling. I haven't told you anyone's secrets but my own—and that is how it should be.

The H Chip

I AM A HYPOCHONDRIAC. I've been one ever since the sixth grade, when I asked my friend Alison if she thought the lump on my neck was a brain tumor (it was a pimple). It didn't help when I acquired a handed-down Peace Corps manual "What To Do Where There Is No Doctor" and began self-diagnosis. The manual was full of fascinating facts, such as the caution that it is useless to put a dead snake on a snake bite in the hopes of curing it. It also warned that you should never wrap a wound in dung. Of course these weren't things I had any intention of doing! Unfortunately, the manual also had tips on differentiating gall bladder attacks from heart attacks—something I mulled over for hours. It was ridiculous to pore over this—not only wasn't I a doctor or even in the Peace Corps, but I lived in a modern city with a hospital and healthcare. But I was hooked on the adrenaline rush of self-diagnosis, and continued hypochondria. I soon graduated to the Merck Manual—where I found I had diseases both common and rare—at least in my head. It is probably good I didn't go in for psychiatric disorders, or I might be in worse shape today.

Now, unfortunately for me, the web provides unlimited opportunities to search out the symptoms of disease. I went so far as to attempt to diagnose my cat. I decided she had diabetes. Luckily for her, I also took her to the vet—who, trust me, did not attempt to diagnose based on a web site. He actually weighed her and did blood work. (She had a mild thyroid condition.) My friend Kathleen and I share this predilection for uneducated diagnosis. We often call each other by the honorific "Doctor" as a joke—and presumably to bring each other to our senses.

My sister Susannah says I need an H chip—one which screens out sites hypochondriacs like. This would be the equivalent of parental controls—although of course the only immature person who can't be trusted that I'd be controlling would be myself. Unfortunately, this hypothetical H chip doesn't yet exist. But my sister's joking suggestion gave me pause. Maybe the real disease I had wasn't beri beri but . . . hypochondria!

I'm afraid I have taken this one step further. Searching on "hypochondriac" I found a quiz to find out if I am one. At first I was really happy—I was going along and scoring one hundred percent to questions such as "I often think I have a rare disease" and "I frequently check myself for symptoms." Then, alas, I started to score in the negative, particularly to such questions as "I go to the doctor frequently" and "I go from doctor to doctor trying to get a diagnosis." The truth is, I hardly ever go the doctor. I go for my annual exam and on the occasions when I am actually sick. I'm a little afraid of going to the doctor on the off chance that I get discovered as a hypochondriac. My doctor is a no nonsense woman. I like and trust her, but I'd be humiliated to run to her with my hypochondria. So maybe I'm not a hypochondriac at all? The quiz suggested that my score indicated I had an anxiety disorder rather than true hypochondria. Oh well, now I can start searching on A . . .

Being sensitive to disease isn't all bad. My husband Rich once had an infected finger I ordered him to treat immediately—once I saw the red streaks growing up his arm. I broke through his male medical denial—and probably saved him from a serious situation. Quick work on my part saved one of my cats from a potentially fatal infection. And where my daughter is concerned—I think nothing of calling the pediatrician at any hour. But this of course isn't hypochondria—nor is it believing I am a doctor. As long as my interest in disease makes me quick to take care of my family and pets and get them actual help—rather than just being quick to worry—there is no problem.

Americans have been called a nation of the worried well. We're assaulted by health information—every magazine has tips on disease prevention, television commercials now sell prescription drugs for what ails us. I decided to fight my hypochondria on two fronts. The first is spiritual. I remind myself that no one will live forever, and that my ultimate fate is not in my own hands. I try to trust in a higher good, and, most importantly, remind myself that while the future is unknown one thing is sure: obsessive worry will make me crabby, neurotic, and maybe even ill. The second approach has also helped. I concentrate on a healthy diet, exercise, and meditation. I figure that if I'm going to pay attention to myself it should be positive. So instead of asking myself—what is that symptom—I substitute—should I go to the gym or do yoga today? And it is helping—at least until I get that H chip.

In Search of Heroines

I WAS LYING IN THE BATHTUB in my mother-in-law's house when my then ten-year-old daughter Isabel pounded on the door. "Mom," she yelled "you have just got to let me read to you about Eleanor Roosevelt!" We'd bought a book about Eleanor at the FDR monument earlier that day. There is no monument to an individual woman in our nation's capital, but part of FDR's sports a realistic statue of Eleanor and a tribute to her. Now, after a day of sightseeing, I was soaking in an attempt to escape the heat of D.C. in August, but I resigned myself to the usual maternal fate that no place is truly private, pulled the shower curtain closed, and hollered "Come on in!"

My daughter read me highlights about Eleanor Roosevelt. I was touched because she had been a heroine to both my mother and maternal grandmother as well. Hillary Clinton may have championed her to the current generations, but originally Eleanor Roosevelt was extraordinarily loved for her support of the downtrodden by women just like my grandmother—hard working, with little formal education, but fueled by dreams.

But what actually impressed my daughter most was the following fact read aloud with great emphasis: "Eleanor Roosevelt earned more money than her husband!" This was thrilling news to a contemporary girl, who'd been raised by a woman—namely me—who may have talked a little too much about women's earning power or lack thereof.

As a girl, I took my heroines where I could find them. I read the biographies of famous women, gobbling them up, looking for clues to a life more expansive than the view from the fifties suburbs where I was growing up. Among the Americans, Harriet Tubman dominated my imagination. At night before falling asleep I too crept along a darkened plantation, whistled for those who had been waiting, led them to freedom. As a Jewish child raised on the Book of Exodus, I loved that she was called "The Moses of her People." Joan of Arc was inspiring too, although admittedly even farther out of my frame of reference. But she and Harriet Tubman had several things in common: they wore men's clothes, they carried weapons, they fought oppressive forces, they led people to freedom.

Years ago, my friend Sarah Lovett called to say she was leaving a book on my porch for me to read. It would provide some relief, she said, from hectic daily living. Since Sarah herself is a writer of dark and terrifying suspense novels, I expected a cliff hanger. Instead, with a bright cover adorned with an old-fashioned little girl, was a copy of *Anne of Green Gables* by L.M. Montgomery. I read every word of this tale of an orphan raised on Prince Edward island, and Sarah was right—it was as entrancing as it was relaxing.

I'd never read Anne as a child, but I had certainly devoured *Little Women, A Little Princess*, and *The Secret Garden*. In fact, I was happy to reread these classics as an adult, and delighted when my daughter discovered them. Why, I wondered, did these literary heroines still touch me? As a rule, they lived in a world where women could not vote, enter the professions, or go to college. These heroines knew little about sexuality or feminism, and they were immune from the problems we think of as contemporary, such as divorce.

When she was about nine, Isabel loved both the little princess and the girl in the secret garden. Both books feature heroines who are displaced and orphaned. "A Little Princess" is banished to a garret in an evil boarding school, while the secret gardener comes alone from India to a house Gothic enough to be in a Bronte novel. Although both heroines are just little girls, they are also heroes in the mythic sense. They are like figures in fairy tales, speaking to us on the level of our hopes and dreams. Forced to rely solely on inner resources, they are helped by servants and animals, while being potentially victimized by adults in authority. And both triumph, gaining families, riches, and a sense of harmony restored to their worlds.

My daughter has never lived in a garret, but she has certainly experienced loss. And any little girl from time to time feels persecuted or misunderstood by her parents and the adult world. I remember sitting in bed reading late at night when the rest of my family was asleep, experiencing a cocoon of silence that I could never find during the day. And reading of how the garret was transformed into an Arabian Nights wonderland by a secret benefactor gave me an image, a role model even, of the transformative power of both the imagination and of kindness.

One of my favorite heroines was Nancy Drew, of the mystery series. Although no expounder of a cause, Nancy still had charisma. She could solve any crime, had a cute roadster car, two sidekicks, and a boyfriend, as well as no mother (often a plus in my imagination), and a father who doted on her. The series was written by several authors, and has changed with time. The Nancy Drew of today is a contemporary high schooler, with perhaps more in common with Sabrina the Teen-Age Witch than with the sleuth I knew. But still, her image remains: competent, clever, in charge of herself.

I've never met an adult woman who hadn't wanted to be Jo, the feisty, literary one among the four sisters of Louisa May Alcott's *Little Woman*.

Nineteenth century books are as full of "broken" families as any problem book for kids today. Jo's father is temporarily, if almost conveniently, gone to fight the Civil War. Here again, a feminine world is left to its own resources. But one of the wonderful things about *Little Women* is that no one is alone—Jo has her sisters, the neighbor boy Laurie, and a mother who is a passionate advocate. And although the novel is essentially Victorian in its sensibility, it is hardly pabulum, addressing anger, death, poverty, jealousy, and a host of social ills in an unflinching manner.

My daughter and her friends have had more to choose from. If I had seen *Crouching Tiger, Hidden Dragon* , it would have fueled my imaginative life for years. My daughter liked the movie, but it wasn't as striking to her—she has already had images of strong women to choose from. When I got older, I still searched for American heroines. My mother dutifully drove me to piano lessons every Wednesday. I hated the lessons but liked the drive, particularly as it always took us past the handsome white house that Elizabeth Cady Stanton had once lived in. My mother and I invariably exclaimed over it—she was our favorite of those who'd fought so hard for women's suffrage—in part because she'd raised an enormous family while doing it. And when Sacajawea appeared on the dollar my daughter and I both rejoiced—I'd loved Sacajawea my whole childhood.

My heroines were as real to me as people I actually knew. But the truth is, I was a little afraid of Eleanor Roosevelt because of something my mother had once told me about how the first lady had made surprise visits to the poor and downtrodden. When my mother's house was particularly chaotic, with screaming children and a pot of sauce boiling over, I was terrified Mrs. Roosevelt might drop in, decide we were poor, and induce the federal government to aid us. I don't think I realized she was no longer living and in general had not made surprise visits to the suburbs. Indeed, Eleanor Roosevelt remained a minor goddess of housekeeping in my mind for many years. I'd make the bed just in case she popped in for a surprise visit.

Heroines give us part of ourselves. They allow us to aspire, and they inspire us. I learned a great deal about self-esteem from reading *Little Women*. Jo March didn't have to worry about saying no to drugs, or about the transmission of AIDS, or teen pregnancy. But frankly, I'm sure she would have done just fine even in our confusing modern times. She knew how to earn a living, follow her aspirations, be charitable, marry for love, and respect herself. I couldn't ask for more for my daughter. To my mother's mother, Eleanor Roosevelt cared about the disenfranchised, she stood for justice and freedom as surely as the Statue of Liberty. My daughter loved her also for her accomplishments, her personal independence. And my house is never tidier than when I expect an unannounced visit from her.

Up At Night—Again

WHEN I WAS A TEENAGER, I sometimes used to run into my mother in the middle of the night. If I came home late from a party or even got up to go to the bathroom I'd find her, wafting about the house in a robe and nightgown. She didn't seem to want to talk, nor was she particularly concerned about my whereabouts. She was just up. It was an odd image, one I soon forgot.

However, when I reached my mid-life and the same age my mother was as she roamed the night, I also found myself awake, often jolted out of deep sleep by a hot flash or a sharp stab of anxiety. Something calls to me to wake up—and I do. Like my mother, I might check to see that the stove is off, or simply stand for a moment and look out the window. My mother favored pretty, old-fashioned nightgowns with lace and flowers and a wrap robe. I'm more apt to be wrapped in a bright piece of fabric I got in Hawaii or flannel shorts pajamas printed with coffee cups. But I know the expression on my face—perplexed, almost worried, a look of vigilance—is the same as hers was.

Once before in my life I was awake in the quiet hours before dawn, nursing my infant daughter. Then, my thoughts were all on motherhood, and the bond between us. I certainly didn't enjoy being awakened periodically by a hungry infant—one I soon realized had been born on the smallish side and therefore took weeks to acquire the weight necessary to sleep through the night. Still, I adored her, and once I'd staggered up I was content to be with her. Someone needed me—profoundly, intimately. The day she could eat mashed banana and drink out of a tippy cup wasn't one of pure joy for me—I knew the early days of mothering her were over.

My daughter was born in dead winter, and I'd often nurse her in the living room with the window blinds up. I loved to look at the great blue spruce tree which dominated our front yard—a protective grandmother spirit of a tree. Its boughs were covered with snow, and when the moon shone the yard was so bright I could see shadows. My daughter and I were in a world of our own—a shadowy world of moonlight, snow, and comfort.

Now I am awake again at the "hour of the wolf" but for a different kind of reflection. The middle of the night is not just a peaceful time, it is also a somewhat frightening one. Alone and undistracted, my thoughts turn inward as I experience the stage of life I'm at, quite different from that of a young mother. I'm undeniably middle-aged, and my daughter is on the verge of adulthood. I feel poised on the brink of change, as are those I love. I think about aging, and feel a certain loss. I certainly won't have any more children, and all the excitement and potential of the childbearing years will soon be behind me. My daughter is closer to the legal drinking age than to birth.

When I look out the window, the grandmother spruce tree is gone. The tree died after several years of intense drought in our region. The tree man who took her down speculated that the tree had been a potted Christmas tree, planted midway in the last century. He counted the rings—just over fifty. The tree was the same age as I was. I'd thought the tree would be there forever, but I was wrong.

The yard looks quite different now. After the tree died, the portal—the adobe porch—collapsed under its weight of years and rotten beams. A lovely renovation job gave us a more airy porch, with elegant wooden columns. The yard changed from shady to sunny—cholla cactus burst into crimson blossoms, vinca flowered blue. Three volunteer piñon trees had sprouted by the spruce's trunk. Apricots seeded from over the neighbor's wall. It is a different view I look out to now in the middle of the night.

When I talk to my friends, I discover that most of them are up at night too. We cite our hormones, our fears, our stress. Jokingly, someone suggests we hold a symposium at 2 a.m.—we're all awake anyway. But much as I love my friends and rely upon them, I don't want to talk to anyone at 2 a.m. I relish the peace and quiet, even the tinge of sadness that solitude brings. When my daughter cried for me, I woke bolt upright. I knew why I was awake, that I was needed, had a job to do. Now I can't help but think that the same is true, even if the purpose is less obvious. I'm not feeding a hungry baby, but I'm nourishing some part of my hungry soul. And like that baby, my middle-aged soul is growing and demanding. Maybe soon it will be a toddler, ready to explore on its own, and even ready to sleep through the night. But until then, I'll look out over my front yard at night, missing the spruce, watching other things grow.

A Daughter's Boyfriend—A Mother's Mistake

I'VE TRIED TO BE A GOOD MOTHER of a teenage daughter with a boyfriend. I've tried to be supportive but unobtrusive—neither too lenient nor overprotective. But it appears I've made one big mistake. At least that is what my dad told me, and he raised three daughters. "You should never have learned his name," my dad said. "He is just an hombre, nothing more."

That was my dad's policy when we were growing up, and who could blame him. His first three children were daughters—looking cute as a stairstep trio in matching outfits in the family album. But soon enough we were teenagers, and to my father that meant close to a dozen years of scraggly fellows ringing the doorbell, taking us out, hanging about, and generally worrying him. And so he feigned indifference—and maybe even had it—claiming he wouldn't learn any boy's name until the boy had been around for at least a year. Otherwise, he was generic, or as my father who was fond of the Spanish language, would say—just an *hombre*. The flow of boyfriends starting with me and then my sisters wore down even my father's system, and he experienced boyfriend exhaustion. By the time we brought home the men we would marry, my father greeted them with a touch of fatigue. Although my father proved a close and supportive father-in-law to all of his daughter's husbands, he first had to recover from the instability of boyfriends.

My mother's system was different. She took to feeding all boyfriends their favorite foods. She inquired about their lives and grew involved. And then she would have her heart broken when they vanished from the scene. It didn't matter if we broke up with them or they with us. She'd just grown atttached—and to this day will sometimes reminisce wistfully about her favorites.

Of course, being my mother's daughter, I didn't realize that the boys who started appearing in my daughter's life were just hombres. As soon as any callow fellow showed, I instantly offered him something to eat. I asked about school.

I offered hospitality. It was a set up for heartbreak. Soon I cared about this particular boy. I was glad when they seemed happy, sorry when she dumped him, glad they got back together, worried things were on the fritz . . . I had to remind myself to concentrate on my husband (who had actually once been a boyfriend/hombre and who still remembers the delicious boysenberry sherbet my mother stocked for him) and to stop caring about the romantic lives of high schoolers.

But I've also given this some thought. I can't be completely impartial, because any boyfriend and I have something very deep in common—we both love my daughter. Our love may be very different in kind, but I can't help but empathize. For example, we both know just how cranky she can get if her blood sugar is low and that she needs to eat immediately. We've learned not to take this crankiness personally, but to steer her towards a snack. We both want her attention—and her admiration. Of course her boyfriend doesn't care if she cleans her room or does her homework—and a mother is not a date! But we both are focused on her in a similar way.

My friend, the poet Joan Logghe, wrote a touching poem in which her daughter starts off as a baby, crying in the playpen, her arms outstretched for her mother. As the poem continues, the same daughter is now pulling her boyfriend down the driveway with the same intensity. My daughter sometimes wears her boyfriend's coat or puts on his huge sneakers. I can't help but remember a time when the person she wanted to dress up as was me.

My mother's life improved when she aquired sons-in-laws. She could assume they were permanent—or at least not coming and going with the regularity of boyfriends. She could feed them and inquire about their lives and not then feel foolish that she had bothered to learn their preferences, problems, and proper names. I have only one daughter, but I've had to learn from both my mother's and my father's systems. Spontaneous interest is natural to me, but I can see my father's point. In some way he was emphasizing to us that these boyfriends were ours to have and worry about—not his. They were essentially hombres until they became family members, at which point he could relax his guard and let them in.

My daughter's boyfriend has been around a lot longer than a year. I couldn't help but learn his name, his taste in video games, his hair color penchant, and bits of his childhood memories and his personality. He can't be a pure hombre to me—but neither is he an adopted son. Yes, I'm rooting for him, but really only as long as it suits my daughter. So he is somewhere between a son-in-law and an hombre . . . .perhaps the most suitable place for a boyfriend.

Time Is On My Side

EVERYONE I KNOW COMPLAINS about not having enough time. My sister Susannah likes to fantasize about what she would do if she had another two hours a day—exercise more, read, garden.

"What would you do?" she asks.

"I have all the time I need," I say.

Oddly, this isn't really a sociably acceptable answer among my friends and family, a group of hard working women, many of whom are moms. Time stress is a reality of our lives, but is also something we boast about—or at least enjoy complaining about.

I really do have enough time. That's because I subscribe to the words I once heard a Zen Master say: "Time is me and you." Time is in my body, heart beating more slowly than that of my cats or guinea pigs, human time. I have time for two simple reasons:

    1. I do not watch television

        and

    2. I have no work ethic.

I have never watched television as an adult, nor owned one. This gives me many more hours in a day than most of my fellows. Basically, it is the extra two hours a day that my sister craves. To be honest, I don't live a particularly media pure life—we rent videos, I love to go to the movies, and I'm happy to watch basketball in a sports bar. But television is an endless supply of time-killing programs, and avoiding television creates free time. One problem with television is that it kills time—a half hour passes quickly—while something like hanging laundry slows time down and five minutes feels substantial.

Number one is my first time trick. Now I also have number two. Paradoxically, this comes from an awareness of the brief, fleeting nature of life. When my first husband Robert died at the age of thirty-six, I lost all interest in appearing to be a hard-working person. I was too blown away by grief. I no longer put up a front of a work ethic. When I recovered from the most acute throes of grief, I kept my new habit. I try to work as little as possible. I live and support my share of the family on a modest amount of money. I never—never—pretend to be busy or working when I am not. Instead, I lie down.

We like to keep busy in part because most of us judge ourselves and others by our level of activity. My sister doesn't want to look selfish or slovenly. If her husband is cooking dinner, she is apt to try and look busy as well. I, on the other hand, am not inhibited in my urge to stretch out on the couch, stare into space, and at most exert myself to stroke the cat a few times. The negative side of this is that I do indeed have a reputation among my friends and family for slothfulness. But it is just this apparent wasting of time which gives me such a sense of leisure. Lying on the couch I can brood, mull, daydream—and time passes slowly. Fifteen minutes of this is like a mini-vacation; and, in any case, the cat doesn't seem to mind.

So one of the reasons that I feel I have time is that I am well-rested. I sleep nine hours a night and nap every day. I no longer lie about this. But although most of the world seems to feel that napping is best done in kindergarten, reports express the fear that we, as a nation, are vastly under-rested. There are even quizzes to take to find out if you are sleep deprived (naturally, I am not, but my fellows are). Lack of sleep causes everything from car accidents to decreased productivity at work to just plain crankiness. I was thrilled to see a study claiming that people who slept less than six hours a night had shorter longevity than average. (It didn't exactly say excessive napping increased life expectancy, but I can hope.) Scientists counsel short naps to readjust the chemistry of the brain and allow for better functioning. Any cat who can catch a mouse is proof that being well rested increases speed and prowess. However, although the experts may have now convinced you to try to rest up, a lifetime of habits spent in productive activity may interfere with your ability to just lie down and snooze. Still, it is worth a try—and an easy place to start in terms of acquiring a more leisurely sense of time.

In addition to being well rested, one of my most useful time skills is that I also strictly limit how much I will do each day. Basically, I never do more than ten things a day. I make a list, with just ten things on it, mostly the usual obligations: drive daughter to school, teach class, take out recycling, write book review, etc. I do these things, then I lie down. I also have to confess that my other great time management skill is that my husband Rich does all the food shopping and a lot of the cooking. But if you can't acquire this time management trick, you can still do the others.

My lifestyle of having time can be a strange and secretive one. For example, my friends regard me as a busy and productive woman. I have written many books, I teach a heavy load at the Community College, I write columns and articles, I travel for work, I raised a child, I am married, we entertain, travel, and keep in touch with large extended families. But there are many—many—things I do not do. I have no beauty regimen. I am a poor housekeeper. I do little volunteer work. My yard is funky. I don't subscribe to newspapers or magazines. Still, every day, I have enough time to nap, read, walk, and to waste many hours talking to my friends on the telephone. The truth is, I do what I like, and I avoid other things as much as possible.

Because I don't try to save time; I enjoy squandering it. One paradox I've noticed is that the more so-called time saving devices we use, the less time we seem to have. A case in point—my household has no dishwasher, no microwave, and no dryer. We all spend leisurely—wasteful!—minutes with hands in soapy water, or painstakingly hanging wet laundry on the line. Rather than contributing to time stress, these activities are meditative. Hanging laundry slows me down, it takes me back to a simpler time, it reminds me of funny stories of my grandfather's long underwear that froze solid into anthropomorphic shapes in the winter, and it puts me in touch with a time when no one knew the word "multitask."

There is a downside to having enough time—boredom. Hanging laundry is a lot duller than watching a sitcom. Perhaps one of the reasons we often avoid large chunks of free time is the boredom factor, or worse, the vague anxiety that surfaces in quiet moments and that can turn into full blown what-is-the-meaning-of-my-life existential despair. We fill our quiet moments just to avoid it. But introspection is fertile ground. It is worth hanging out with that boredom to discover what is underneath—creativity, inspiration, a relationship to yourself.

Recently we had a group of friends over for a backyard brunch. Close friends stayed late to help us do the dishes—all the while remarking on our lack of dishwasher. We did the dishes, cleaned the kitchen, joked and bantered, and our kids played on the lawn. Our friends stayed much longer than expected, and when the chores were done an unplanned serious discussion sprang up, and we all sat down to problem solve some issues in our work lives. It was a fun, and then productive, time—a spontaneous event after the party. Our friends parting words were: "Get a dishwasher!" But I couldn't help think that with a dishwasher none of this would have happened, and that with a dishwasher I wouldn't have had this balmy Sunday afternoon that seemed to stretch on forever.

Sad to say, no one truly admires my time management. They either assume I'm lying and am just as busy as they are, or figure I am a bum, and no asset to society. The truth is, this system is so easy to follow, but I can't get anyone else to do it. Maybe that is because they say they need time. I, however, prefer to spend it.

If you need some help, try this:

How to Get Started—Some Tips on How to Rest Up

Find Your Power Nap Spot

Just as a shaman supposedly will find a power spot before he or she will settle into a room, a cat will also scout out the best nap spot. You should do the same. The nappers in my family (perhaps my condition is genetic) are divided into two camps: couch nappers and bed nappers. My father ritualistically puts on his pajamas, draws the blinds, and gets into bed for his daily nap. My mother scorns this, preferring to sleep fully clothed on the couch in the midst of activity. I take after my mother, perhaps because even in our need for rest we are mommy-tracked, ready to surface and find a lost pair of sneakers or help with homework. To find your power spot, take a quiet half hour when you are alone in the house. Try couches, bed, armchairs, recliners, until you find what works best for you.

Equipment

Luckily, there is very little additional equipment needed to start resting today. I find a soft, small blanket is useful for warmth, and a favorite pillow might be kept at hand. Some people like the prop, or pretense, of a fat dull book or newspaper to nap beneath, but this is only for those timid about their right to rest. If you feel the need of an authoritative aid, go for the totem animal of rest: grab a nearby cat and let the feline help you pace yourself for a long nap.

Nap With Authority

A desire for rest is all well and good, but you may have to fight for it. After all, no one tells adults to lie down because it is nap time. I find it best to simply announce, in a bold tone, that you are going to rest, and should not be disturbed. A bit of mystique might help as well, you might be a bit reverential, as if you were a monk announcing you were off to tell your beads, or that as a super athlete you were now training for the triathlon. If those around you do not immediately respect your nap boundaries, forget your power spot for the moment and firmly close your bedroom door, saying only at what hour you expect to resurface.

Credit Your Rest

The next time someone tells you look glowing, don't credit your new haircut or gym. Instead, give credit where it is due—to your rest. The phrase beauty sleep says it all. Rave about your new regimen, and talk freely about how and when you nap. I've been well rested for extreme states such as labor and delivery as well as more mundane situations such as giving a lecture or a flooded basement. In each situation I've been extremely grateful that at least I wasn't exhausted to begin with. It's unlikely that in our work-oriented, sometimes puritanical, society that rest will ever attain the status of making money, or fulfilling New Year's resolutions for diet and exercise. I don't expect my social profile to go completely from lazy bum to rest guru, but if it does I'm sure to thank the real experts, my cats, for showing me the way.

Fun

WHEN I WAS A CHILD, I sometimes wondered at my mother's peculiar habits. She often would take circuitous routes on her daily rounds of car pool and errands just to stop and admire other people's houses and gardens. In spring, she had her special azalea viewing spot and, in autumn, she preferred certain streets for their maples. My mother would sometimes even vanish mysteriously for a few hours at a time, saying she was going to the public library to read the fashion magazines. From the ignorance of childhood, I frankly never understood why she would need a break from a household of four children and the care of four aging parents and in-laws.

It was only when I found myself as an adult woman, parked between work and school, admiring a stunning bed of some stranger's deep blue iris that I flashed on my mother and understood what she was doing. My mother always tried to build tiny refreshing breaks into her routine. It was one of her virtues that she could turn a visit to the Five and Dime into an orgy of delights worthy of Tiffany's. I learned from my mother, and like her I call these breaks "a small good time."

Today's families often seem to have lost our sense of fun. We work hard at jobs, school, extracurricular activities, and hobbies, and then we play hard at expensive high maintenance vacations. We seem torn between between two extremes—the rushed life of routine and fast food dinner and then major fun, costly, and potentially exhausting events. However, in nature, all families play. Watch a group of otters, who have more fun in ten minutes than we do in two weeks at Club Med.

Some of the most fun, in the simple old-fashioned sense, that I've ever had was as the member of an informal club. The Tuesday Club, as it was called, was composed simply of me, my friend Hope, my pre-school daughter Isabel, and Hope's son Reuben. The purpose of the club, which usually met Tuesday afternoons, was to give two moms some company and a break from cabin fever in rainy and snowy weather. Our goal was to have fun—fun that all four of us could agree on, fun that was free or very cheap, and fun that was nearby. The Tuesday Club taught me a great deal about how to seize the moment—and enjoy it. We followed railroad tracks into the woods, climbed through river bosques, or sometimes just went to the mall to look in the windows of the pet store. A favorite memory is an impromptu parade we created at Sears. We'd gone to admire the tractors (something I would not normally think of doing), found some American flags in passing, and just started marching.

Although my own childhood was full of low-key fun, I always wanted a special event I never got—a cat's birthday. When my daughter's and my two new kittens turned a year old we invited Reuben of the Tuesday Club to come to a party. We wore party hats, gave the cats catnip, and ate a chocolate cake. The cats hated it—and fled at the sight of candles and loud rendition of "Happy Birthday." But we enjoyed it—mostly because were having a party for no good reason on a school night.

My mother was very attuned to the seasons when I was growing up. Every spring, she'd pack us into the car and drive around the neighborhood, exclaiming over the blossoming trees. We had flowers in our garden, too, but there was something illicit and delightful about appreciating other people's. My mother would savor the first fruits of summer—cherries or a peach—with full appreciation. I can still hear her exclamation of "delicious!" During the winter holiday season we were back in the car, cruising towns for miles around in search of the best Christmas lights and displays. Ever since my daughter was a baby, it has been second nature for me to drive around oohing and aahing at fairy lights and farolitos. The passage of the seasons is an opportunity to enjoy ourselves. This kind of fun has an almost spiritual element, as it connects us to the cycle of the year.

The Tuesday Club pretty much dissolved when the youngest members went to school. But Halloween was our reunion. We followed the same routine: everyone, including adults, dressed in costumes. We went out for an early dinner at a cafeteria or salad bar to prevent complete bingeing on candy. Then, in my mother's tradition, we went to our favorite Halloween neighborhoods—the ones with the best displays of pumpkins and skeletons, haunted houses, and flickering graveyards. Again, it was a bit of an adventure to be off our own turf. But in this day of mall trick or treating and worry about razor blades in apples, our Halloween was a return to an early time.

Most fun of all is the mystery walk or drive. Start out with your child on foot or in the car. Let the child decide where to go—literally saying "turn right," and "turn left." My mother would drive us like this in the car to our great excitement. My daughter and I explored our neighborhood on foot this way. It created adventure from the mundane, and made us feel like explorers.

One of the major keys to having fun is to simply announce—to yourself or others—that fun is about to begin. It is possible to approach even the mundane this way. And fun may simply reside in the details. One little girl I know, when asked what she'd liked best about the Grand Canyon, said "the squirrels." Childhood memory is laid down in microcosm, it is the small things that are fun. Couples therapists and marriage studies show surprisingly that happiness in relationships is measured not necessarily by compatibility or "work" on the big things but by how much people enjoy each other. The same is true for parent and child. Your children, most of all, will thank you for slowing down and exploring the world with them.

Some years after the Tuesday Club, I once found myself in a car with Hope, who was taking a very odd route between the grocery store and her house. We went down a winding dirt road I didn't even know existed, past some old-fashioned adobes with walled gardens. "This is my secret route," she explained, "I take it a few times a week and look at what's happening—house renovations, gardens." Hope was on a system like my mother's—and enjoying it.

So take a different way home. Find the street or neighborhood or view that refreshes you, and then indulge in it. All of these things will give you a break from existing mental habits. A yard of daffodils seems to wipe the dust of daily seeing from your eyes. No one need ever know about your small good times. But you'll know, and even grow to be a connoisseur of looking at the world freshly again.

Motel Oasis

RECENTLY, A FRIEND OF MINE AND I found ourselves snowed into a motel at one end of a closed mountain pass. I was traveling for work, she had come along for company. Sitting in that motel room, contemplating the indoor pool, looking forward to eggs and home fries for breakfast, we suddenly realized we were in a state of bliss. It had taken a lot of arranging to get away from home, and now we were temporarily stuck, and totally happy. Truth be told, I was less than three hours away from home. And the motel—although pleasant—was just a basic roadside accommodation. But I was as delighted as if I had suddenly found myself in Club Med in Tahiti.

I have always loved hostelries of any sort—I just love sleeping under a roof not my own and not having to make the bed in the morning. Of course I like a grand hotel—the Plaza in New York or the Biltmore in Phoenix—but it is rare that fate and my budget allow me true luxury. So I'll take my fun where I can find it, even in an anonymous chain. Of course what I really like is not being home. I have no domestic chores, the phone doesn't ring, and I can indulge in television, while at home we have none.

When my daughter Isabel was a year old, she weaned herself. I was both happy and sad that this part of mothering was over; and I was also desperate for a taste of solitude. I went to a motel about two miles from home, with strict instructions to her father to call if he needed me. He didn't. For twenty-four hours I slept, lay in the bath tub, and watched nature shows. It was as salubrious as a week at the beach—I was completely refreshed.

Motels signal solitude, anonymity, and the sense of being on a journey. No doubt this can be depressing to some, but for me a motel is like a yoga retreat—a way for me to touch base with myself. I've lifted weights in motel rooms, danced to rock and roll tapes, written poetry, made collages, and given myself facials. I don't even need Virginia Woolf's prescribed room of my own—a motel room will do nicely.

Not everyone shares my love of the low-key motel. I have friends who have wrinkled up their noses and said "You're staying *here*? Why not go someplace nice!" But luckily the friend I was snowed in with that night shared my appreciation, and was happy to settle in and relax. We had talked for uninterrupted hours in the car, and by the time we had gossiped in detail about even our most far-flung acquaintances we felt free to ignore each other and read in bed.

I'm glad too that my family shares my love of motels. We have our routines. My daughter chooses a bed by bouncing, my husband unpacks the cooler as carefully as if we were embarking for the South Pole. I enjoy the temporary household in a classic motel setting, even with odd floral bedspreads and hideous oil paintings of sunsets. But the truth is, for me the ultimate use of a motel is pure solitude. I experience a sense of enclosure and privacy that a hermit might feel in a woodland hut. The environment is mine to command—whether television program or silence. I'll squeeze my motel retreats out of trips for work, but I'll also sometimes just book myself out of my life and into a cheap motel by the airport for a day or two. I'm not really going anywhere—just inside my own head, an oasis for me alone.

A Spending Diet

I LOVE TO READ SELF-HELP BOOKS on how to simplify my life. But, I don't always practice what is preached. In fact, I can sometimes even fall into the trap of buying an expensive hardback on spending less money rather than taking it out of the library! With this in mind, I decided to go on a kind of spending diet. For thirty days, I wouldn't spend any unnecessary money.

This resolution led to a flurry of discussions in my house. My husband Rich—who believes I am profligate—was delighted until he realized that once again we didn't agree on the concept of "necessary." He gloated: "So you won't be eating out all those fancy lunches?" Lunch! I hadn't even thought of that. Lunch is my main source of social life—and a fair amount of business, too. He lost interest when I decided to limit the experiment to purchases of objects— books, clothes, etc. Maybe he didn't realize what a major change that would actually be for me.

My rule of thumb in defining necessary was that if something like my car brakes or kitchen faucets broke, I would definitely fix them. If I was due for a haircut, I could get it. But I couldn't buy a half dozen fancy hair products just to see if I liked them. Although every friend I mentioned this to immediately had a slightly different definition of necessary, if you want to conduct this experiment, write down your own contract with yourself. That way you won't cheat too easily. To keep on track, I started writing everything down. Here are my notations:

Day 1: Went into the grocery store on a vacation trip to Colorado to buy a loaf of bread. Did *not* buy a *People Magazine* or the cute Hawaiian shirt for the great price of $4.99 as I've got about 25 aloha shirts in tropical prints in my closet. Felt sad but virtuous.

Day 2: In stationery section to buy necessary office supplies. Did not buy socks, as I often do when I go into this store. Sad not to buy green socks with pink cactuses on them, but cannot justify "needing" such an item.

Day 4: My friend Ana, whose clothes fit me and who has great taste, gave me a hand-me-down end-of-summer dress in brown and white checks. Very cute. Almost as good as shopping.

Day 5: Should not be reading Judith Krantz's autobiography which is making me sad I can't buy things like diamonds and houses in the south of France. Poor choice for austerity budget—but I bought the paperback before I started this.

Day 10: This seems to be getting easier. I was in a great museum gift shop and wasn't even tempted. Have I have found the secret to frugality?

Day 13: A dear friend of mine told me she furnishes imaginary houses in her mind—"buying" things she sees to fill it up. Great substitute.

Day 21: Was at a sweet crafts fair and REALLY wanted to buy something. Did not get rose quartz earrings. Did not even get some half-priced pottery dishes, despite desire to support local crafts people. I asked everyone: don't we NEED these dishes? Everyone said: NO.

Day 24: Reading lots of clothes catalogues, earmarking favorites, and telling myself this will all soon be over. Is this cheating?

Day 26: Something horrible has happened. I fell off the wagon completely. Without thinking, I went into my favorite magazine store and bought the one thing I needed for my class—then bought $20 worth of magazines I wanted! Feel like a dieter who has just eaten a box of chocolate chip cookies. What happened? I couldn't be pure for even thirty days. But I'll continue to the end.

Day 27: Will be very virtuous—enter no places of retail but rather work on the yard and go to the gym.

Day 31: The urge to spend a little something is irresistible!

The experiment was actually more difficult than I realized. I noticed that I often bought myself "just a little something" to cheer myself up on an irritating day or to celebrate a small triumph. No wonder I fell so unconsciously off the wagon amidst the temptation of a rack of magazines—I probably should never have even entered the store. But like a real diet, or health regimen, failure is an inevitable part of it—starting again is what is important.

I did not conduct this experiment to save money, but as a form of self-discipline. Still, it was alarming to note just how much cash is actually frittered away each month on cute socks. It was informative to learn that should I need to cut back my budget I can still eat lunch out and repair my car while saving a large chunk by not spending on fripperies. Of course, once the experiment was over I went out and bought a very cute shirt covered in turquoise flowers, just because I could. But I certainly didn't need it.

A Shared Account

"I WANT TO FEEL CLOSE TO YOU," my husband said.

I smiled, envisioning a weekend a deux at the hot springs. But just as my imagination was providing me with a romantic soak, I was brought back down to earth.

"I think we should open a joint checking account," he said.

I was stunned. We'd been married five years, and I thought we were close! I also thought that our fiscal system was working. Although we were a blended family, our assets weren't merged. We each maintained our own accounts and split the household and child expenses down the middle. It had seemed to work. What was different now?

Well, recently, I'd wanted to talk about future plans. Every so often topics would come up—should we buy a bigger house, move to a different city—that seemed to stall with a lack of shared financial vision. I kept wanting to talk about things like inheritance and retirement but my husband Rich had demurred, saying we didn't have a shared fiscal system. Actually, it was a bit more than that. We weren't sure we had shared fiscal values either.

Rich is the Ant of the fable—the one who saves. He is thrifty, cautious, precise, good with numbers—and let us admit it—he earns part of his living as a bookkeeper. Now I'm not really the opposite. I'm very budget conscious and generally thought of as fiscally responsible. Its just that, marriage being about contrasts, I'm careless Grasshopper to his Ant. I don't save as much as he does, I love to spend money on myself and on the family, and I care less about small economies. I also don't balance my checkbook. But before you call the Fiscal Police, I would like to say in my own defense that I know exactly what is in the account and don't bounce checks. Still, I knew Rich thought this was unbelievably slovenly.

I wasn't always the Grasshopper. In my first marriage, I was the Ant. My first husband, Robert, had a cheerful disregard for money—at least other people's.

He once ran up an enormous balance on our credit card and then declined to pay any of it. I was afraid to share money with him—as he simply blithely spent it. His good humor was great to live with, but his fiscal irresponsibility was a nightmare. So I actually had no experience of shared money management in marriage.

"I'll feel close to you if we have a shared account," Rich said. "And then maybe it will be easier to talk about larger topics." I thought this was just more bookkeeping, but I gave in. We opened the account. I also suspected that perhaps it was a test—the Ant checking to see if the Grasshopper would blow the budget on fripperies or tickets to Rio. I began to pay a few of the household bills out of the joint account, and yes, I balanced the checkbook. It seemed boring, if uneventful.

A month or so later I found myself weeping hysterically over the joint account. Here was the problem—Rich likes to save, not spend. We continued to deposit into the account until it had a large balance. Only a few expenses were authorized and the account continued to grow. Now it was more of a savings account than a checking one! And my personal monthly budget was totally shot, because I was essentially paying into the account and then also paying bills directly.

As I sobbed, Rich put his arms around me and announced, "But I do feel close to you." Maybe he didn't realize how deeply I cared about my budget—an Ant trait like his. Maybe he was happy I'd balanced the checkbook. We decided to give it a few more months.

To my surprise, things improved as we went along. It appeared that Rich was right. By seeming coincidence, we had a fruitful discussion about saving for college tuition. Rich had some good ideas that we could put into action. The next time we looked at the joint account we were able to agree that we wouldn't let it build up over a certain balance—it would be checking, not savings. We paid for a holiday vacation out of it. Then, we hit a glitch. I had entered some numbers—gasp—in the wrong column. Although Rich pointed it out gently, I felt concerned for my Grasshopper reputation. Then Rich noticed that he himself had failed to enter a deposit—or maybe not—where was that pesky deposit slip, and how come . . . So it appeared even the Ant could make an occasional mistake. And these mistakes were quite minor—but I was relieved we had both made them.

Truthfully, I don't think Rich and I are all that much closer. My final analysis is that we are only closer in the way people can be by being courteous towards each other's needs—in this case his need for the account. As for me, anytime the Ant and Grasshopper go to the hot springs together, I'm content.

Four Generations of Philanthropists

I CAN STILL REMEMBER the first time my father gave me my allowance. I was in grade school in the early 1960's, and although the weekly sum was modest, it seemed lordly to me. Unlike that of many of the other children I knew, the allowance was not an implied payment for chores. My father had a different attitude—in our house, you did your chores simply because you were a member of the family team, not for fiscal reward. And you received an allowance for the same reason—the family's resources were there to be shared.

My father instructed me on my first lesson with money. "There are three things you can do with money," he told me. "You can save it. You can spend it. You can give it away. And I suggest you divide your allowance into three parts and do just that." This was certainly unusual advice, and one which emphasized charity. But it was just that third option that caught my imagination. I saved and saved—my goal was to join the Bronx Zoo as a member, all by myself. I knew that members got great discounts, but the thing that really drew me was that members got invited to a special tea with a resident *platypus*. A platypus, I knew, was a rare, endangered species from Australia, that looked to be part mammal, part fish, part duck. I was captivated. The platypus became my motivation. I did save some of my money to buy myself toys, and I did squander a bit, but I saved my third, motivated by both genuine philanthropy and by something which even big-time givers cannot resist—the promise of a great party.

Just when I reached my goal, after close to a year of quarters, my grandfather—my father's father George—got wind of my horde. Grandpa George was a highly charitable giver, but he was also a bit of a personal tyrant. Grandpa George decided I should give my money to Israel to buy trees—his favorite cause of the moment. I had nothing against trees, but I was determined to aid my platypus. A dreadful scene ensued, in which my grandfather tried to bully me out of money. He managed to get me alone, cornered, at one end of my mother's screened-in porch. My back literally to the wall, he loomed over me like a gangster intent on collecting. When my father burst in on us—appearing out of nowhere like a hero in a white hat—he made my grandfather back off. I had been intimidated, but determined to hold on to my money to give as I chose.

I got my garden party with the platypus. It was everything I had expected: ladies in big hats, large white tents, and the platypus swimming serenely in a special tank. I can still remember the plates of tiny delicious cookies scattered about. It was the first time I ever tasted the ones shaped like chocolate leaves. I was as happy as if I had personally funded the entire event. I remember people smiling at me too—I must have been the youngest member there.

Children are naturally charitable, particularly when it comes to money. A child may not want to share his/her toys, but be interested in giving away the contents of the piggy bank to a homeless person. A friend of mine told me that his children didn't even realize until they were six or seven that money was used for anything else but charity! As parents, we can easily foster this impulse, in part by not interfering with it. We need to let go of our own fear and clinging around money—for example, by thinking "Well, I could never give away a third— or a tenth—or any—of my own income."

A combination of animals and charity is irresistible. My daughter's religious school class spent a year raising the money to buy a goat for a faraway impoverished rural family. The goat was so vivid in my daughter's mind—the milk it would give for the children, how the neighbors would buy the cheese—that she was highly motivated to donate.

My father taught me a double lesson. He gave the allowance freely—it wasn't earned. As an adult, I've worked for a living but frankly some of the most demanding things I've done—raise a child, keep house, care for a sick person, be a friend—have no financial reward. No one will pay us to be part of a family, or part of the larger family of society or the natural world. And through giving my allowance I became a true philanthropist—powerful and benevolent and brave enough to stand up to my grandfather on behalf of a platypus.

In Search of Romance

It seems that almost any time I am in a group of women talking about our lives one of the main things that everyone complains about is lack of romance. We all say we want romance, and are disappointed that we don't get enough. We want it from our husbands particularly in certain gestures we find lacking—the gift of a single red rose, the candlelit dinner, the heart-shaped box of candy. But is our longing really one that can be satisfied by clichés or tokens that are rarely forthcoming? And is romance really something that can be generated for us by another person?

As a rule, the women I have known have spent an inordinate amount of time turning boyfriends into husbands. My friends and I started out as teenagers who couldn't discern too easily the difference between bad and good boyfriends. But we soon learned. Bad boyfriends were cute but unreliable; good boyfriends were reliable and hopefully cute. We got burned by bad boyfriends, rejected useless ones, then finally settled on Mr. Excellent Boyfriend and married him.

However, "they lived happily ever after" is a phrase found only in fairy tales. My friends soon started complaining that Mr. Excellent Boyfriend was now Mr. Husband, and therefore unromantic. He no longer wined and dined them, but instead left socks on the floor, watched hours of sports on television, worked too hard (insert your favorite complaint here.) Then to a woman we spent fruitless effort trying to turn our spouse back into Mr. Boyfriend, usually through whining, complaining, and nagging.

Part of the problem is that we expect romance from the relationship arenas of our lives, but don't practice it anywhere else. Romance is essentially about risk, unknown situations, and a heroic self-image. Poet Lord Byron going off to fight for Greek independence was romantic—driving a carpool usually is not. But there are many ways to discover romance within our lives, and a romance which is deeper than a hastily bought box of chocolates on the way home from work on Valentine's Day.

Several years ago, I had a highly romantic experience that had nothing to do with the man in my life. My friend Sharon Niederman, who was on a travel writing assignment, invited me to take the train and stay at La Posada in Winslow, Arizona. This had many of the basic elements of romance—leaving home, a leisurely form of transportation, an unfamiliar destination. La Posada hotel was built when travel was still romantic (slow, luxurious, a bit uncertain, as opposed to the fast food approach of airplanes today). I added my traveling outfit that could have passed for Edwardian—a black velvet hat, long skirt, long coat. Getting off the train late at night and walking to the lit up hotel was the essence of romance—the night was freezing, the hotel looked inviting, there was a a speck of the unknown thrown in to add excitement. It was perfect.

It is a psychological truism that if a man and a woman face a life-threatening situation together they are apt to fall in love—that old shipwrecked on a desert island routine. That is because adrenaline—excitement—can be perceived by the brain as falling in love. In contrast, most long-term relationships basically appear to lack certain prerequisites for romance—they are not mysterious, and they are not dangerous. And yet, if we truly regard another human being, his depths are unknown to us. At one time, my husband Rich and I were trying to plan our goals for the future. We did this over a series of lunches out with each other. Lunch, to me, is more romantic than dinner in that it is less predictably a stage for a date and has an oddly clandestine appeal. Trying to work out some conflict, we made a list of things were felt we couldn't discuss with each other. I was startled—actually shocked—by what was on his list. I could never have predicted his topics. I suddenly saw this very familiar man as an unknown—and fascinating—quantity.

After my visit to La Posada I decided to go back, this time with Rich. To create an aura of romance about it I gave him an unexpected gift certificate for a night there—forcing us how to figure out how to get out of town. I knew he would love it—the trains passing in the night, the faraway feeling of it all. I also invited my daughter and a friend of hers. Family life and romance are usually set up in opposition, but I knew that these two teenagers would find their own adventure in exploring the hotel, having their own room, sitting in front of the roaring fire. My husband and I did indeed have a wonderful time with each other. But part of the success, I think, was that the emphasis was not on us having a programmatic romantic experience, but on a sense of adventure.

One useful way to approach romance lies more in accepting a person's style than in hoping and complaining. For example, on Valentine's Day when my husband Rich gave me a bunch of asparagus I was disappointed. I complained to my friend Sharon, who saw it otherwise; "How romantic! The first asparagus of spring!" she said. Suddenly I could appreciate the gesture. Men do many things for us—often day after day—which we take for granted rather than as the expressions of love that they really are. When a guy puts air in your car's tires, brings you coffee, is nice to your mother—see these things for what they are—selfless gestures of love.

September 11 brought a heightened sense of the ephemeral into many people's lives—but the same can be true of simply observing life itself. Most of us cannot make it to middle age without both experiencing serious loss and perhaps the gift that loss can bring—a heightened awareness and appreciation of the present. If you look at your significant other as if you might be suddenly parted, feelings of love cannot help but rush in. The essence of romance with someone else is not a predictable setting such as a candlelit dinner—and the essence of bringing out your own romantic self-image is not a bubble bath. You need to go deeper than these easy ready-mades and seek your own true nature. Allow yourself to take some risks—climb the mountain, go to an unknown destination, or just try a food or book that is unfamiliar to you. In this way you build up your muscles for romance.

Romance might even be a gesture of altruism—writing a check for someone in need or helping in a more extreme life-threatening situation. My friend Devon almost lost her husband to an acute infection. The ICU is not touted as a romantic setting, but his recovery there was probably the greatest moment she had in twenty years of marriage. She told me, "We'd thought of going to Europe for our twentieth anniversary, but frankly even Paris can't compete with what we experienced together." Life, beneath even the most predictable routine, is unexpected, startling, even scary. Allow yourself to feel this—and you will also feel the romance.

Family Is Where We Find It

EVERY OTHER THANKSGIVING, I find myself in Las Vegas, Nevada. Las Vegas certainly does not provide a homey holiday atmosphere. However, among the anomalous scene, of dancing show girls with cleavage covered in glitter and dancing fountains I find myself eating a Nebraska-style Thanksgiving dinner with "relatives." My second husband's brother's wife's mother, Gwen, is our hostess, and she provides us with a turkey, creamed vegetables, and pies straight out of the heartland.

Somewhere perhaps there is a tribal society that has one word to describe my relationship to Gwen. However, in America, with its emphasis on the nuclear family, we actually aren't related at all. Still, she and her family are important to us. My second husband's brother's wife's sister's adopted daughter is my daughter's "cousin."

"You and Lyn aren't really cousins," I insist, but the distinction is meaningless. The two girls adored each other from the time they met. Enormous upheavals brought them together. Lyn was airlifted out of Korea as an infant and adopted. My daughter's father died when she was young and she has been raised by her stepfather. Her step-uncle married the woman who was Lyn's adoptive mother's sister. If you can't follow this, it really doesn't matter. Lyn and my daughter just *are* cousins. They erroneously believe this is because they sort of have a first cousin in common—my husband's nephew. He is actually my daughter's step-cousin, but I don't know why I bother to unravel this at all.

What is interesting here is that neither of these girls lacks for "real" family. Lyn has several cousins; my daughter has six first cousins on my side, all younger than she, all clamoring and adoring. In fact, its an overwhelming scene when we're together. But she and Lyn aren't content to be friends, a bond which though as intense as family is purely volitional, chosen, not given. They feel the bond is given—so they are cousins.

The so-called blended family is nothing new. Fairy tales like Cinderella tell us of the ancient tension between stepparent and child, the ancient problem of who rates as a first class family member and who is relegated to the outside. The shock that widespread divorce delivered to our notion of family is something we are still reeling from. I was born into a world where almost no one got divorced; by the time I was a teenager many of my parents' friends had split. My daughter grew up in a world where divorce was a commonplace for children—both feared and accepted. But our fate as a small family was a more ancient one—we lost our husband and father to death. This has made me sensitive to all the good that stepparents do, despite their maligned status. Perhaps I come by this honestly. My mother's father's mother died in childbirth. His father married her sister— a custom among European Jews. My grandfather was raised by his stepmother cum aunt, who was actually the only mother he ever knew. He had adored her, and transmitted to me a sense of gratitude he had about her care, perhaps more intense because he knew she had in part chosen him.

When my daughter had her bat mitzvah, that quintessential family event for a Jewish coming of age, her family was indeed there. My parents were there, her father's mother was there, and her step-grandparents were as well. Gwen was there too of course. If she introduced us to Vegas buffets and farm style creamed peas, then we introduced her to a sort of Hippie/Jewish/Santa Fe-style bat mitzvah. I looked up and saw her singing along, gamely following the unfamiliar service. Here was our family—beyond blended, and into the new millennium.

Meditations of a Daughter-in-Law

I HAVE SPENT MUCH OF MY LIFE being a daughter-in-law. And there are two things I don't like about the role ... the need to act in a conventional manner and the feeling of inevitably being an outsider. Despite a changing world and feminism, the role of daughter-in-law always makes me feel old fashioned. I think of it as a social setting in which I must be polite, somewhat deferential, and serve snacks. It is a situation where of course I am more visible as a wife and mother—less so as a professional or autonomous woman. There is also the sensation of being an intruder into a family system—no matter how welcome a one. I don't necessarily understand the system for washing the dishes, or the jokes. This isn't *my* family of origin, where I'm clear on how much to tease, and whether or not to mention how much something cost. In my husband's family I have always felt a bit exotic—my family is a lot noisier, nosier, and argumentative than his. We're not as thrifty, or as good kitchen managers. Sometimes I feel like a parakeet that had flown into a flock of more sober birds.

All this changed when my 80-year-old mother-in-law Claire entered hospice care. An extraordinarily lively lady, despite various ailments, she was vigorous in her old age. She loved to sightsee, travel, and make and sell her pottery. Then, she was diagnosed with a serious cancer that soon looked to be terminal. She had numerous operations, bouncing back from each one so quickly it amazed the doctors. But eventually the disease overcame her, and nothing more could be done.

My husband and I flew out to Washington, D.C. to help care for her, little realizing just what a roller coaster this would be. Throughout the years of visiting, I knew my in-laws loved and appreciated me, as I did them. But I also had quirks that were odd to them: I could never keep up with them sightseeing, I needed time alone, I liked to nap, and I was perhaps frivolously interested in clothes and shopping. Now, the butterfly was about to turn into Florence Nightingale.

My in-laws hadn't wanted much nursing care, not exactly realizing just how difficult Claire's final days would be. My father-in-law was the primary care giver, changing sheets, washing her, giving medication. We soon fell into a natural team effort. My husband ran the house, kept us fed, rushed out for supplies, manned the phone, and tried to cajole his mother into a sip of liquid or a bit of applesauce. I was my father-in-law's assistant. As things progressed, my role evolved—I called 911 when Claire fell, I was up all night when she began to bleed, I talked to hospice and took instructions at dawn. I transcended many of my own limitations and was able to do things I wouldn't have thought possible from a standing start.

Of course this was in part because I wasn't just some flighty creature. My in-laws didn't necessarily know this, but my past included years as a suicide/drug hotline counselor, a stint doing hospice at the start of the AIDS epidemic in San Francisco, a long night helping my godson to be born, and of course being a mother, with its attendant all nighters, ER visits, and just plain getting over squeamishness. One thing that helped me enormously throughout was my ability to treat Claire the way I always had. She was quite alert until she died. In the last few hours of her life she could barely speak but asked for her comb and brush. She managed to whisper that it was on the wicker table. "Thanks," I teased her, "for telling me. I can never find *anything* in your clutter!" She cracked a smile and I brushed her hair.

In the middle of a particularly bad bout of pain and bleeding, I was trying to get Claire to turn over. "Yay! You did it," I said encouragingly. She looked up at me and said poignantly— "if someone had told me we would be in this position I would never have believed it." The positive surprise was not only that I was able to care for her but that she allowed it graciously—and that I had never felt closer to her. In the last five days of her life her needs and concerns were my world. People expressed admiration afterward, but frankly it was easy. She needed me, and we could both be ourselves. I didn't have to be polite or conventional, and I was in as far as possible with the entire family.

After Claire died, my father-in-law asked me to give one of the eulogies at the funeral. Claire had no daughters, and so I decided to represent the women in the family. My sister-in-law Leslie had written Claire a beautiful letter and I got permission to add many thoughts from it into the speech. I also quoted my daughter, Isabel, who said something both touching and original. "Claire was my step-grandmother," she'd said. "You know what to expect from a grand-mother, but a step-grandmother . . . now that was a nice surprise." In caring for Claire, thinking about her life, and speaking about it, I got to know her in a way I never had before. And to appreciate our relationship as well as mother-in-law and daughter-in-law.

How to Talk to a Widow

THE DEATH OF A SPOUSE is one of life's harshest calamities, and the situation can be made all the worse by social awkwardness. Most people just do not know what to SAY when confronted by the reality of death, and a new widow is in no position to teach them. However, there are some guidelines to follow that will turn a condolence call from something that might offend or upset the bereaved to that which such a call should be—a show of support and affection. My experience was as a widow, but the same can be applied to widowers, of course.

When my husband Robert died after a long illness, I was confronted with the fact that many of our contemporaries had little experience with death. And many of them were terrified of saying the wrong thing to me, or simply did not know what to say. My experience—and the experience of other bereaved people I talked to—led me to the first rule of the condolence call: It is better to say something rather than nothing.

I ran into an acquaintance on the street months after Robert died who looked none too pleased to see me. "I wanted to say the right thing—the perfect spiritual thing," he said, "but since I couldn't figure out what it was, I just didn't call." There is no need to make this mistake. No one can say the perfect thing in this situation. Frankly, I was delighted to have people simply say: I'm sorry. Children, as always, will sometimes show an honesty that adults lack. One of my daughter's closest friends, aged six, made us a card that said, "I'm sorry that your father and husband died." For me, that said it all.

Talking about the deceased person is also something that widows usually find comforting. After all, he is foremost in their minds. Far too often, those paying a condolence call jar if a widow so much as mentions her dead husband's name. But the wound is fresh, and needs to be expressed. Most widows appreciate any sort of reminiscence. Oddly enough, it was the UPS delivery man who said something I will always cherish. Robert had had several home businesses and used UPS a lot. The delivery man expressed shock over his death, and then said simply, "Your husband was a very nice man who was always smiling." That meant a lot to me. I also appreciated memories of any sort that people shared with me—even lighthearted ones, like the friends who told me that Robert was always a great source of juicy gossip or that he was an inspiration to stop going to boring dinner parties.

Unfortunately, the list of don'ts in this situation is considerably longer than the list of do's. I was startled by many things that people said to me, and every widow has a horror story about someone who said the exactly wrong thing to her. But rather than be struck mute by fear of a faux pas, the condoler should simply avoid the following.

Do not, under any circumstance, pry into a widow's affairs that you were not privy to before her husband's death. Numerous people asked me if I was financially secure, planning to move, or to sell my house. Since these people were neither my accountant nor my realtor, and most particularly people I would never discuss my financial affairs with normally, the inquiry felt rude and invasive.

I think it best not to comment on a widow's appearance. Over and over, people told me I looked well. I was horrified that they were judging my looks during a crisis. Other widows feel an implied criticism here, as if their friends are actually surprised they haven't lost their looks in one fell swoop. I eventually realized that people were probably just saying they were relieved to see me. It would have been easier to have them say that.

In general, remarriage is also not an appropriate topic. Still, particularly for a young widow with children, the issue of the future cannot be avoided. I was very cheered and amused by stories my friends told me about widows they knew who had bounced back. I heard tales of a great aunt who made a fortune after her husband's death, and who would report her profits during graveside visits. And I enjoyed the accounts of an old-fashioned cousin who remarried again at eighty in a scandalous seven months after being widowed. I have to admit, though, that friends who were bewailing their single state had less than the usual sympathy from me in the weeks after I was widowed.

If you still are unsure of what to say to a widow and feel inhibited with words, a gesture, no matter how small, works wonders. Death is one situation where actions do speak at least as loudly as words. A casserole of course is the traditional gift, but I was greatly helped by legal advice (from an attorney, not an acquaintance), gardening, housecleaning, childcare, and a friend who did all my laundry. One friend told me she had been dreaming about me, and instead of giving it an airy-fairy interpretation said, "This dream means I should carpool your daughter to school," for which I was extremely grateful. Practical help may not seem romantic, but for a widow not only emotionally prostrated but practically overwhelmed, it is a godsend. One suggestion—do not limit help to the few weeks after the funeral. I was exceptionally grateful to people who took me to lunch or my daughter to the movies months after the death when we still needed support but were less apt to get it.

Of course, in a condolence call, as in all important situations, try to be yourself. The awkwardness of the situation need not make you awkward, and any widow will appreciate a spontaneous show of true concern. But remember, a condolence call is not about the condoler—it is for the mourner. Don't burden the new widow with your own tension and doubts about the situation. Show you care. If you can, let the widow unburden herself, reminisce, cry, or simply sit quietly. You don't have to say the perfect thing. Sometimes just listening is enough.

Helping a Child through Grief

GRIEF IS AS MUCH A PART of a child's experience as of an adult's, and yet adults—parents in particular—are often uncomfortable allowing a child to grieve. When my daughter's father died when she was six years old, I was forced to confront this directly. As her mom I had usually been able to make everything all right—from changing a diaper to kissing a boo-boo. But this was one enormous problem that I could not make go away. Instead, with the help of professionals, I found that the best thing I could do was listen.

One out of every twenty children in the United States today will lose a parent to death before he or she is twenty-one. Modern medicine, and contemporary attitudes, view the death of younger people as an aberration, but despite this many children are forced to confront the death of a parent. And this is not the only loss that children face. There is the separation of households in divorce, the illness and death of grandparents, the loss of a beloved pet, and even a change in friendships or school.

It is a truism—if a completely false one—that children cannot really grieve. Perhaps it is the adults who find comfort in the idea that children don't "understand" death as if we as adults truly do. Children grieve according to their developmental age. For children under five, a kind of magical thinking may make them believe that if they behave in a certain way the dead person can come back to life. It is important with younger children to reassure them that death is no one's fault and could not have been prevented by the child.

Anne Maskalenko, a registered art therapist who works with children in the schools and individually, says that "grief is a process, not a feeling, a process that takes place over time. Our culture doesn't give it enough time, there is avoidance in our culture." Grief can include anger, guilt, blame, and terrible sadness—all uncomfortable feelings that we as parents often wish would simply go away.

The adult rituals did not seem to work for my daughter after her father died. She did not want to attend the funeral or memorials, although I gave her that choice. Instead, she naturally evolved her own rituals. She built an angel with the art therapist she began to work with. The angel went next to her bed, beside a picture of her father. Every night before falling asleep she talked about her dad, sometimes saying she missed him, sometimes remembering funny stories. At times the ritual seemed perfunctory, at times it evoked tears. But by creating a space to talk, my daughter knew that it was always safe to express her grief. Maskalenko adds: "A child needs to experience feelings as they come up." Therefore, if you are dealing with a child who has experienced a traumatic loss, it is absolutely necessary to create time and space in which those feelings can come up at their own rate.

After her father died I immediately put my daughter in therapy. In our society, therapy itself is a kind of ritual, an acknowledgment that help is needed. When choosing a reputable therapist for a young child, the creative therapies have a great advantage. Expressive therapy, art therapy— these modes allow children to respond on a nonverbal level. In art therapy my daughter built a large bowl and painted a message to her father on it. The bowl was a kind of container for her feelings. She built statues of her father, and eventually an elaborate model of a new house to live in, as her process changed. Working with sand trays is another good technique, where dozens of tiny figures of people and animals can be used to build imaginary expressive scenes. These release what Maskalenko calls "the wisdom of the psyche," or even a child's natural ability to heal.

Anniversaries and holidays can be particularly hard times for grieving families. At my daughter's school part of the Spanish curriculum was a celebration of the traditional Mexican Day of the Dead. The children built an altar and placed on it photographs of anyone they wanted to remember. There were pictures of lost pets, of ancestors, even one of Jerry Garcia. At first my daughter found the celebration painful. But by the second year she was able to enter into it more easily, remembering foods her father had liked to eat, particularly pepperoni pizza.

Judaism encourages lighting a memorial candle on anniversaries and certain holidays. Children respond well to such simple rituals, even writing a letter to the deceased or planting some flowers or a tree in his or her honor.

Professionals agree that children who are not allowed to grieve end up with the problems of unresolved loss as adults. It is important, too, for the child to remain a child, and not become the caretaker of the remaining parent. I asked our family's pediatrician for advice after we were bereaved. A wise woman, who knew a great deal about children and families, she gave me a rather startling piece of advice: "You and your daughter will have to heal together." At first this frightened me—I didn't want to be that linked to a grief-stricken child. After all, I was the adult, wasn't I?

The pediatrician turned out to be accurate. My daughter and I did heal together. I had to learn to listen instead of rushing in with advice and comfort. I learned from her ready ability to create art and ritual. And I also learned from her ability to change. "I still miss Dad," she said, "but I have a happy life." My daughter suffered particularly from an inability to concentrate and learn after her father died. She had trouble getting on with her friends. When I told her I was writing this article, less than a year after her father's death, and asked her if she had any advice. "Tell people that their child might get sensitive feelings if someone dies," she said. Grief is indeed a process, and therefore one which will eventually end in at least its first intensity. My daughter's willingness to grieve wholeheartedly, and her willingness to still love life, were my greatest lessons.

How To Take Advice

MY BEST FRIEND FROM HIGH SCHOOL, Juliet, is now an actor's manager in Los Angeles. She knows a lot more about things like hair and nails than I ever will. Every time I go to visit, Juliet sets to work to improve me. Last time, she painted my nails gold, using at least three nail products. Then she ran something called "curl-up" through my lank hair until it looked better, if not exactly full-bodied. When I came home, my first impulse was to rush out and buy nail polish remover. But the gold looked cute. I was getting compliments. Juliet had been giving me beauty advice since we were fourteen. Now she'd even given me a bottle of gold polish. It was time to learn to take her advice.

I realized recently that I am surrounded by intelligent, thoughtful women, each with her own special areas of expertise, from accounting to cooking. My friends often offer a gentle observation or two on my various problems, and while I smile and nod, I don't always leap into action. That's because I, like many people, have a fear of taking advice. I come from a bossy, nosy, butt-insky subculture, whose members were constantly giving me and each other unsolicited, unwanted, and imperfect advice. Maybe your relatives told you to never wear brown, or to find a man to support you. Well, shades of brown have changed to match your eyes, and support is something you don't think of in financial terms. Or maybe perfectly sound advice, like your mother's "don't slouch" or "don't squint, you'll get wrinkles" was repeated so often it could only be called outright nagging.

But there is a difference between commands, even if slightly disguised ones, and the gentle suggestion of a friend. I realized that while I often solicited advice, I usually ignored it. Planning a trip to Hawaii, I complained to my friend Carol that my weak hip made it difficult for me to hike over lava out to see the volcano flow.

"Get a pair of hiking boots," she suggested, looking at the flimsy pair of Chinese slippers I usually favored.

"I hate them. They're so clunky."

"Miriam," she said distinctly, "hiking boots have changed since you last looked—which I suspect was about twenty years ago."

"And expensive ... "

"Less than a hundred dollars," she insisted. "Go to the mall."

Carol was right. The hiking boots were light, affordable, and much more suited to climbing over lava than my embroidered slippers. I'd asked, and although it had taken an effort of will to take the excellent advice offered, I was improving.

Part of my resolve to take advice was predicated on separating good from bad. My first rule of thumb was to double check if I had asked for advice, as I did from Carol. I do have various friends, who despite their other virtues, share a bad habit of bossy, unsolicited advice. When you get such advice—on child rearing, your career, or on not wearing khaki—you can pretty much discard it politely. This advice serves the giver, not the receiver.

A gray zone is a friend who has listened patiently to your problems, and has been implicitly asked to comment. Juliet has heard me complain about my hair for over thirty years. Perhaps she thought it was time to take action, and perhaps she was a little tired of the complaining. In cases like this, where a friend rushes in but isn't exactly uninvited, run the advice across an acid test of what works for you. Ask yourself—does this advice seem sound, does it reflect my needs, is it being offered impartially to help me rather than to express the advisor's needs. If you can answer yes, go ahead and take the advice.

Also, if you need expert advice, go to the expert. I wouldn't take medical or serious fiscal advice from a friend—unless that friend was a doctor or stockbroker and was charging me for it. But for those small but crucial areas of life, like should I get my car detailed, cut my bangs, or re-tile my kitchen, friends are invaluable. My friends have rehung my paintings, landscaped bits of my garden, gotten me a new accountant, and told me to drink soy milk. And yes, although my nails are no longer gold, I have a great pair of hiking boots and a bottle of curl-up.

A Currency of Favors

I RECENTLY SPENT A HECTIC MONDAY afternoon doing a favor for a friend. I picked her daughter up at school, drove her to gymnastics, drove back across town to pick up my daughter, then back to gymnastics, then back to my house, and so on. This particular friend and I have had an elaborate system of favors we've done for each other over the years, and we keep a kind of informal score. Most of it has involved childcare, and we both like to be in the black—to be owed—because it means we can take a grown-up night out on the town.

But this particular Monday was different. My friend had jumped on a plane to travel two thousand miles, despite her dislike of flying, to tend to an old friend of *hers* who had just been released from the hospital after surgery for a very serious condition. As I stalled in traffic, fiddled with the radio dial, and asked children if they had all their belongings, I felt connected by invisible threads to an unknown woman I had never met.

This web of women's friendship functions profoundly in our lives, but often on a subliminal level. I have become increasingly aware of the currency of favors the longer my friendships last, and the more stages they pass through. Years ago when my friend Hope went on maternity leave and I took over her job—a problematic one involving the managing of several chaotic projects—she thought I was doing her a favor. I, however, felt indebted because she had given me work. When she sent me an arrangement of iris at the end to thank me, I felt I should have been the one to extend the thanks.

We offer our friends compliments, advice, and amusing stories—but the currency of friendship involves concrete things as well. My friend Debora can still remember how when her son was born I and another friend, Joan, washed her dishes and tidied her apartment. This physical gesture meant a lot to her. Then again, I felt I owed her because she was there for me when I was in labor—she had even run out to get me some mints in the middle of the night. And no doubt she felt she owed me for all the great hand-me-down clothes I had passed on to her—tons of rayon, silk, and cotton separates over the years. The list goes on, and I'm glad it does. For since the score can never be evened, I'm inspired to continue giving and receiving.

We've all had unfortunate experiences of friends who don't respect the give and take of a mutual friendship. The neighbor who borrows the lawn mower and doesn't return it until the first snowfall isn't apt to become a trusted friend. I once had a very problematic friend who took offense easily. We were having lunch and I picked up the check. After I paid, she took that moment to tell me we could no longer be friends because I had appeared to be sympathetic to her landlord in a quarrel they were having. She stalked off—leaving me with my change in hand. For a moment I felt utterly wretched—and I couldn't believe I had paid for her chicken Caesar salad only to get dumped. Then my heart lightened—what a relief to not have to quarrel with her anymore!

Then there are some things that can never be fully repaid. When my first husband died, several of my friends moved in with me and my daughter and took care of us sequentially. Their support truly saved us. On a trip to Asia, I bought all of them the most exquisite jewelry I could afford—jade pendants of Kwan-yin, brilliant coral pieces hung on knotted strings. Was the jewelry payback for their kind deeds? Of course not—it was simply a token of gratitude, an acknowledgment, and a thank you.

When my friend returned from her trip I got a report on how her friend was doing post surgery. She was recovering—and her courage and perseverance were inspiring even second hand. "Well, I owe you," my friend said happily. She'll gladly drive my daughter or take her for a sleepover and then feel she has money in the bank with me. Somehow I don't want to collect on this one—would rather leave it as a good deed. But I know that it is also important between us to keep the currency of favors going—a trading back and forth on a score that can never be truly even—and thank goodness for that, because it keeps us all going.

Fear at Fifty

I AM AFRAID OF A LOT OF THINGS. My fears include black widow spiders, assembling electronic equipment, driving long distances alone, and speaking in public. Some of these fears are things I have to face—some I can simply avoid. For example, I always delegate installing the new phone machine but I've learned to tolerate driving through vast expanses. As a teacher, I lecture every day with just a bit of nervousness—but brushing a black widow off my leg still remains one of my most terrifying moments. I don't like to feel stuck in my fear, though. That is why, as part of my fiftieth birthday, I decided to face one of the most frightening things I could think of—a gun.

Guns scare me for two major reasons: they are lethal, and they are totally unfamiliar. So when I turned 50, I asked my friend Hope to show me how to shoot a gun. Hope has a ranch, good common sense, and an orientation towards safety. She has owned and shot guns most of her life. I knew she wasn't afraid of them, and would make the perfect teacher. Why did I want to learn to shoot a gun? It was because now that I was irrefutably middle-aged, I wanted to address the thing in my life that has plagued me the most—fear. So I picked something I was afraid of and decided to confront it directly.

Hope was delighted to introduce me to something in her world, and took me to the local shooting range. I'd dressed carefully for the occasion in jeans and boots and Hope was pleased I wasn't in one of my usual flowing ensembles. "I'm glad to see you're not wearing a caftan!" she commented. So I was in the right outfit, but just touching the gun at first was frightening. She showed me how to open and load it, and safety precautions for handling it. We put protective equipment on our eyes and ears. But nothing had actually prepared me for pulling the trigger. The sound and the smell—and perhaps most of all the sense that a truly lethal weapon was in my hands—were deeply scary. My feet started to sweat until they were slippery. My mouth went completely dry. But here was the interesting thing—we weren't done yet. I shot one round, and then shot another despite my soaking feet. This was a good experiment in continuing to function while afraid.

There are times in my life when I've appeared to be brave—and when I've actually been brave. I've nursed the dying in hospice, and I've helped a baby to be born. I'm basically good in medical situations, and I'm not particularly squeamish. One incident in particular brought this home. My family was checking into a motel when the owner had a seizure. Her husband became hysterical and screamed at us to call 911. In an altered state of calm, I called for help, stayed with the woman, and talked to the personnel. My daughter commented: "Mom, you were so calm—and I've seen you totally hysterical over little things."

The truth is, I can sometimes become more anxious over a broken sink than a real life crisis. But the reason I was calm was that the seizure didn't frighten me—I simply wanted to help. I wasn't being brave, just genuinely unfazed.

The same was certainly not true of the shooting range. My aim wasn't very good, but I did keep shooting. I proudly brought home the target, which was mostly near misses, as a trophy of overcoming my fear only to have my daughter say, "Well, at least you scared him!" And no doubt I simply frightened my target off. But I also scared off one more thing—some of my fear. By the time Hope and I were in the parking lot I felt just fine and pleased with myself. She was even surprised to hear I'd been so terrified. And when she invited me to shoot with her again some time I knew that if I did it, it might be fun but it wouldn't be the same. I wasn't actually interested in owning a gun or becoming proficient. I had just wanted to overcome my initial fear, and not be paralyzed by it.

What I learned from the shooting range is that guns actually are frightening—after all, they are lethal weapons. But there is a difference between healthy respect and terror. After this, I started to wish I could get every friend I had to help me do something scary. Devon, who was a strong swimmer, could take me out beyond the Atlantic breakers. Nancy, who worked for the coroner's office, could help me confront death. And maybe an entomologist I know could show me the miraculous side of life in any form—even a black widow spider.

Companion on the Journey

ALMOST A DECADE AGO, my husband Rich and I went on our honeymoon to Hawaii. It was an exquisite trip, of course, full of waterfalls and volcanoes, and the romance of tropical winter nights lit by strings of holiday lights. But there is a little secret about honeymoons that most won't tell—even in our day and age the honeymoon is a way to get to know each other, an entry into married life. And as such, it is fraught with a certain kind of tension.

Rich and I recently took a different, but interestingly analogous trip. We went to Alaska after a difficult year or two of caretaking aged parents and dealing with illness and death. The purpose of the trip was partially to celebrate my fiftieth birthday—with a visit to Rich's fiftieth state—the only one in the Union he hadn't yet set foot in. The two trips had some intriguing differences—and not just the difference between orchids and orcas, papayas and salmon. We knew each other a lot better.

In my parent's generation, a honeymoon was the special trip after a wedding in which a couple could get to know each intimately, away from the eyes of the world. In more contemporary fashion, ours didn't exactly serve that purpose. Rich and I had known each other since we were teenagers, gotten married in our forties, and he raised my daughter. Our honeymoon was actually months after our wedding—the first time we could get away. And yet, certain archetypes run deep. I found myself faintly nervous embarking on the trip, even wondering what we'd have to talk about alone day after day. And indeed, the trip had its moments of adjustment. In Hawaii, we had a fight on one of the most beautiful beaches in the world (I wanted to stay, he felt pressed for time, his mood grated on me, mine on him, etc. etc.). I was sure he was getting us lost down the dirt road to the B & B. He couldn't believe I didn't want to spend hours in the grocery store . . . But the thing I learned on that trip was that it was possible for Rich and me to exist in the present together. We spent days pointing out flowers and views to each other, discussing meals, not looking to the future or even analyzing the past. The memories are among the highlights of my life. And yet, despite knowing each other, we were also newlyweds.

Years of married life passed. We traveled together in many ways. We were in places as mundane as Clovis, New Mexico, and as beautiful as a friend's ranch at sunset. We dealt with unemployment and overemployment. We worked on raising a daughter and doing hospice care for my mother-in-law. We fought about stupid things and important things. And I knew I didn't have to talk every minute.

When we went to Alaska, there was nothing newly wed about us. I certainly didn't worry about whether we'd have enough to talk about. And I was more accepting. I knew by now that one of the ways Rich bonded with a place was by exploring its grocery stores (and the one in Juneau happened to be located with a great view of a glacier). Also, I knew that some of our issues traveling were issues of thrift—his thrift, that is, and my indifference to it. Rich was happiest with picnic lunch, and only one meal out a day. I could accept picnic lunch—particularly when the picnic was on a completely deserted beach surrounded on all sides by majestic snow-covered mountains and flocks of water birds. But I also emphasized that I was planning to eat seafood on every available occasion—expensive or not. The picnic ethos was challenged the afternoon we arrived in Sitka. A shack was selling king crab by the massive chunk, for a reasonable price. We had bread and chips in the picnic bag. Rich waived his rule and we were soon dripping sauce for a lunch that we dubbed best of the trip.

But Rich had accepted me, too. We took a long day's ferry in the Inner Passage. My love of napping is sometimes at odds with his more frenetic pace. I also have a bad hip with attendant pain, that is sometimes relieved only by lying down. As an amazing treat, he booked me a private cabin where I could nap in style. It didn't break the budget, but it was certainly a completely unnecessary luxury. Rich was pleased with himself, too. Apparently the booking agent had been confused—who needs a cabin for the day? "But they didn't know you," he said. And, of course, he truly did. As I lay in my bunk watching islands slip away in the mist, I realized this was one of the nicest presents any-one had ever given me.

Sometimes the concept of acceptance or accommodation may seem too simple-minded. It sounds like pabulum, or worse, a compromise in which no partner ever gets to fully express her or himself. What I learned between Hawaii and Alaska was that acceptance can be a form of enjoyment. There is pleasure in seeing the person you love delighted by something—and yes, it is also possible to come to enjoy something out of our usual spheres of interest. It really is pos-sible for each person to get more of what she or he wants rather than less. And so much the better if you get to eat some king crab on the way.

A Better World

I WAS RECENTLY STANDING in the napkin section of a party goods store when I was struck by the optimistic revelation that the world is getting better. Partially it is because I love paper goods. And paper goods are so much better than when I was a child. Then, it was a thrill to get plates and napkins emblazoned with Happy Birthday. But today I can pick up paper goods seemingly designed by Picasso—or for an English tea party. Standing there among so many brightly colored florals and geometrics, I just couldn't help but feel my world had improved.

It is a commonplace to say that the world is getting worse. From the international situation to individual stress levels—most of us can't help but exclaim that things seem like they are deteriorating. But is this really true? Granted, party items are a pretty frivolous measure. How about something serious—like underwear? For, really, underwear isn't as frivolous as it sounds. In the 19th century women wore corsets so tight that they couldn't breathe, and fainted. Pressure on internal organs could damage them. Women even had surgery to remove their ribs to make their waists thinner. Granted, some of us still go to extremes for beauty, but a general aesthetic of permanent disfiguration like corsets, or foot binding—is mercifully a thing of the past. I can remember my mother in her tight girdle—and how happy she was when she took it off after a day spent in the city. She can still remember the joy she felt when pantyhose were introduced. I remember my own unhappy shock at the constricting undergarments of my early adolescence. And the blissful historical moment when suddenly garter belts vanished as if by magic and were replaced by knee highs, and even better items like footless lace tights and warm ribbed pantyhose. When I took my own daughter shopping for the first time for grown-up underwear I was even more pleasantly surprised— items were in great colors, lightweight, easy to wear. All I have to do is be glad I'm not wearing a corset—or frankly garters—to feel the world is improving.

But enough about the ephemera of fashion. What about matters of life and death to women—such as childbirth? A century ago in the then territory of New

Mexico, it was a commonplace that women made their wills in the last months of pregnancy before they went into labor. Today in the United States, the expectation is quite the opposite. Despite the risks that will always be there, childbirth is no longer the death defying experience it once was. We happily assume we'll live through it—and just as importantly, we assume our children will live too. Not so long ago, women bore many more children than we do today—and lost so many of them. An old graveyard will tell the story, with lots of tiny, poignant tombstones. Now at a distance this just seems sad and unfortunate—but for the mothers it must have created life-long devastation.

Looking back in my own family makes these things tangible. My grandfather's mother died in childbirth; my mother-in-law lost two siblings in childhood. In my own family, the world has certainly gotten better. My grandma Sadie came to America as a young teenager, leaving behind life in a country where she was persecuted for her religion and ethnic group. A story shared by many, but one I try and take time to appreciate. If it hadn't been for her courage, the family would never have survived European history. Neither I nor my daughter would have been born or alive today. Sadie worked hard and had my mother, who went to college. But Sadie herself had no education, and was barely literate. The life lived by her great-granddaughter—in terms of education, travel, freedom, and opportunity, would have been almost unimaginable, but delightful, to her.

In a way, one of the greatest gifts of improved health and freedom is just the ability to enjoy the little things in life. My grandma Sadie adored nice clothes, and she was a fan of fine linens, too. I know that she'd love today's great paper napkins--and that she'd really love to see what kind of young women are growing up in her family. It may be inevitable that we react to the world today with pessimism and a sense of decline. But we need our optimism not just to go on, but to have faith and vision. It helps to think of the women of the past and those in our own families—and to be grateful for what is indeed good in our lives—from our multitude of choices to our underwear.

Ethical Will

WILLS SERVE AS MORE than practical documents—they are also a fascinating record of lives left behind. After all, William Shakespeare baffled posterity by leaving his wife—whom he hadn't spoken to in years—his "second best bed." My sister Susannah was recently amused to find a twenty-five-year-old diary containing a list of where her prized sentimental possessions should go in the case of her untimely (and fortunately not occurring) death. Women in the nineteenth century made wills before the dangers of childbirth—one wrote from out west back to her sister in Ohio that she was leaving her a pair of amethyst earrings should she not survive the ordeal. Wills help us clarify our relationship to possessions and people.

An ethical will bequeaths not money or property to one's descendants, but instead leaves a record of beliefs. It has its roots in Jewish tradition, where a rabbi or other devout person would leave a list of moral instructions to be read after death. Ethical wills have recently become more widespread. They are essentially a way to write a letter to the future, in which you explain what religious, spiritual, moral, and ethical beliefs helped you live your life. When I began revising this essay for this book I was helped by Tres Chicas editors Renée Gregorio and Joan Logghe. They became immediately interested in the notion of ethical will, and so I suggested they write down some of their own thoughts on what they would bequeath to posterity. I've added in their perspectives—and their enthusiasm showed how natural it is for us to want to share our values.

Ethical wills are a wonderful way to preserve family history and personal experience, and are not difficult to write. Imagine if you had a letter from one of your great-grandmothers explaining what beliefs motivated her life. Such a letter would be a treasure—as much or more as an heirloom tablecloth or set of silver. We inherit values in any case. Joan remembers her father: "When my father died I recall the sadness and feeling nothing was left of him and then I remembered his generosity. I must have shaken two hundred hands before the funeral, and knew that he had given and helped people. I felt that was my inheritance from him and hope that I can leave behind generosity of spirit as well."

With this in mind, you can set out to write your own ethical will. It requires no special format, but it will take a few hours of uninterrupted time. You can start it informally in your journal, or put it right on your computer. Just make sure your finished copy is easy to read and clearly labeled—print out a copy and put it in its own folder, the way you would any legal document. The following steps can help you get started on an ethical will. Feel free to be creative with these—they are not a strict set of instructions but rather ideas that may inspire you.

1. *Looking to the Center of Belief.* The way to create an ethical will is by first writing down the central beliefs that have sustained you. For example, I know my own mother has been uplifted throughout her life by classical music and by gardening. She might want to write about creating a beautiful garden on sandy soil at the beach or studying music theory. In contrast, a close friend has always drawn strength from the tenets of her church. I know that an ethical will of hers would concentrate in part on how prayer helped her during a medical emergency. Each approach is individual. For your purposes—identify the things you have believed in and were sustained by. You can start by simply roughing out a list. I know that loyalty would be high on my own personal list. But you can then explore the value of each thing. Although I'm very loyal, I have let friendships go that caused more harm than good. Expand the points that stand out for you.

Renée answered the question of sustenance in the following manner, drawing in part on her training in both aikido and poetry. She says: "Belief in some deeper natural rhythm of the earth and of myself that is beyond comprehension but felt and sometimes known. Belief in transformative experience through the body, what's possible between people through the body. Belief in the power of language to transform. Belief in what could only be described as Eros, as life-preserving quality of body and mind as expressed in love, creative acts, poetry, aikido. Belief in instinct, intuition, cooperation, spirited conversation."

Joan focuses on thanks: "I believe in thanking every night for my life, God or breath or life itself for the day. On the way down to the pillow my head fills with thanks. The pillow reminds me I was alive all day and get to rest."

2. *How Did You Deal With Difficulty?* Every life has had its moments—or years—of crisis, whether financial, emotional, or health-wise. When you were confronted with life's difficulties—what helped you the most? It doesn't have to be a deep philosophical approach; many of us, for example, are greatly helped just by talking with our women friends. As my teenage daughter says of her own support system: "Just talking with the friends is a perk up." Or maybe it was yoga, prayer, therapy, or watching funny movies. Joan adds friends and books and walking. Just having the resources to cope in whatever way makes you a role model for your readers.

3. *What Did You Learn?* Think back over your education in the broadest sense. I have a friend in her eighties who can still remember with great pleasure when she learned to read as a kindergartner—it opened up a whole world for her. We all hope we've learned patience, tolerance, and self-control. But these things aren't all that easy to attain. Are there particular moments or struggles you look back on where you truly learned something about yourself?

For many of us, marriage and relationships have been a strong learning. Renée says she has learned: "That I can be still, live in one place and with one other for many years, call this home. That solitude and companionship can exist under one roof."

4. *What Did You Value Most?* It might seem that we all value the same things— friends, family, traditions—but there is actually a lot of variation in our lives.

Joan's mother was a businesswoman at a time when that was uncommon. It began as necessity, but became an invaluable part of herself. Joan says: "My advice is the same as my mother's—Get an education—and my mother always said, 'A woman needs something to fall back on.' This from a life-long careerwoman. I always say I fell back on poetry, so make sure the pillow is soft and the bed firm." Don't be afraid to write about slightly unconventional things that you might value. Some of us love solitude, others find strength in earning our own money. Our lives are a patchwork of the material and spiritual, the emotional and practical, the adventurous and the mundane. Maybe running a marathon, or just running along the beach, had particular value for you. I recently read an obituary of a very elderly lady who liked "dancing, shopping, and gambling!" Just that jaunty list made me wish I had known her.

5. *What Advice Do You Have?* A friend of mine recently told me that she'd been inspired by an older friend "to choose happiness." What advice do you have for those who come after you? Don't be afraid to be specific and life affirming or even a little bit silly or idiosyncratic here. For example, I will always advise people to spend a little bit of money frivolously on themselves as a way to cheer up. What do you wish someone had told you when you started out in life?

When asked for advice, Renée said: "Live widely and deeply, don't turn away from your deepest desires and urges, look others in the eyes and with an open heart, speak clearly and truthfully what you hold dear, hold many things and people dearly, have empathy for otherness."

To create an ethical will, start by listing various attributes or ideas and then add details to the ones that are the most compelling. Be lavish here—and share what you've learned. This is your letter to the future—you might want to read and update it every few years like a real will. It is a legacy to others, and a way to understand yourself now as well.

Credo

I AM IN A GROUP OF WOMEN self-christened "The Spiritual Sisters." We did this exercise, each person writing down a list of what she believes in and eventually sharing it. Margo Chávez-Charles suggested the credo—she learned it from her sister, writer Denise Chávez.

To write your own, take ten or fifteen quiet minutes. Simply begin each line with the phrase "I believe" and complete the thought. Don't edit or criticize your thoughts—your beliefs may range from the mundane to the philosophic to the idiosyncratic.

Here is mine:

CREDO

I believe the world is neither good nor evil, but a mix

The same for human nature

I believe in Jeffersonian democracy—perhaps optimistically,
but I do

I believe in a more equitable distribution of the world's wealth

I believe it is better to sit than stand for a living—which is why
I am a community college teacher and encourage upward mobility

I believe each person has her or his own karma—and that
I can't do anything about it

I believe I should give charity or do a small good deed
as frequently as possible

I believe that Rich loves me, that Robert loved me, that
my old boyfriends still love me, and that in general there are
many men who could still love me

I believe in strictly budgeting my money

I believe that God responds more to deeds than prayers—
or that deeds are the greatest prayer

I believe in study, reading, learning—for everyone

I believe the life of the mind is a good distraction from suffering

I believe in eating fruits and vegetables

I believe in not wearing a bra

I believe in baseball

I believe it is fine to be fat

I believe the end of the world is not coming any time soon

I believe in the theory of evolution

I believe that marriage is not for everyone and that people
should not try to stuff their individual selves into an institution

I believe that a big earthquake is going to hit California

I believe I can handle many kinds of emergencies

I believe that sex and money are kinds of energy rather than
fixed things that control us

I believe that Beatles' songs have messages directly for me

I believe there are other worlds—other realms of consciousness
than this

I believe I can currently know nothing about life after death

I believe in keeping my passport current

I believe in the mystical power of calendars and seasons

I believe it is good to eat garlic

I believe in my dreams, sleeping and waking

I believe there is vast energy beyond me that can aid me if
I tap into it

I believe in the Zone

I believe I will die

I believe in rock and roll

Consider doing this more than once. For example, it could be done once a year or on an important occasion. Beliefs change, yet remain powerful. A credo is a good way to reflect upon yourself.

Count Your Blessings

WHEN MY GRANDFATHER AVRUM was about ten years old, he traveled for the first time. He'd grown up in the Ukraine at the end of the nineteenth century in a village between Kiev and Odessa. His father had to go to Kiev from the country-side to have a hernia repaired. In the arching train station, my young grandfa-ther saw a strange human sight. There were two people in long gowns and coats, with skullcaps, long single braids, and facial hair. They were merchants from China, but my grandfather—in a world before television, magazines, or many illustrated books—had no way of knowing that. "Who are they?" he whispered to his father. "Are they men or women?"

Before his father explained, he said a blessing, thanking God for creating human diversity. This story came down in our family—and my great grandfa-ther always seemed ahead of his time in terms of appreciating human difference. But that actually was not the case. The blessing he recited is a traditional He-brew one, thousands of years old. The Jewish tradition has blessings for many occasions—from putting on a significant article of new clothing to seeing the first blossoms of spring.

Probably all religions bless food and drink, a good starting place for grati-tude to the life which sustains us. But we can bring more awareness—and much more gratitude—into our lives by the practice of a hundred blessings.

A hundred blessings a day is practice that I first learned in the Spiritual Sisters. At first it seemed somewhat daunting. Could I even come up with a hundred blessings? But I made the effort.

When I started writing my first list, of course the natural things that came up were my daughter, husband, friends, family. But that was hardly a hundred. As I let my mind float over blessings around me I found some very mundane ones—like the fact that my car finally has air conditioning after twenty years of driving around in the desert heat without it, and also a radio, with music to lift my spirits. On a much larger level, I found myself grateful for the freedom in my life as both a woman and a citizen. My list included huge things shared by many and purely idiosyncratic things. I found I was grateful I could vote— and I was grateful for the funny, cawing crows that sometimes swoop into my yard and seem to talk to me. A difficult person I often complain about also appeared on my list. Apparently I had more gratitude here than I was usually aware of.

When you first start out, do write the blessings down for a few days to increase your focus. When you make your list, take a quiet time and sit down with a notebook or piece of paper. Start listing those blessings, and do number them. One blessing soon leads to another. Don't inhibit yourself or judge—these are blessings, after all, not a to do list! If you can't get a hundred all at once, take a break and come back later. You might find yourself thinking about this when driving around town. You'll start to see blessings everywhere. Once you get the hang of it, you don't need to keep writing them down. In fact, if you feel tense or overwhelmed, you might simply count ten blessings to yourself as a quick way to change your mood.

I got so excited about counting blessings that I started to do it in the classroom, too. I was recently teaching a creative writing class to a group of middle school girls. They counted their blessings—charming, funny, universal, idiosyncratic. Many of them included "night" on their list—a time of privacy, introspection, rest, and of course dreams. One girl really surprised me, though. "Diabetes" headed her list. How was that a blessing? She explained: this disease has made me who I am, it has made me understand myself and learn how to take care of myself. I was very touched by her insight—a wisdom usually attributed to a much older person.

I know that when I talk to my friends—and often when I talk to myself—I complain. Problems seem to be the order of the day. We don't usually greet each other with a list of what we are grateful for! And being told to count your blessings in a crisis can often feel like pure hogwash—who needs it.

But the truth is, experiencing blessings can bring us to a deeper level. Appreciating what is good in our lives can make us more ethical and more likely to stand up for what we believe in. It can help us focus on what we care about—air conditioning, crows, friendship.

Miriam Sagan is a columnist for *Sage Magazine* at the *Albuquerque Journal*, and for the book pages at *The New Mexican* and *New Mexico Magazine*. She is a regular contributor to *Writer's Digest.* Her books include a memoir, *Searching For A Mustard Seed: A Young Widow's Unconventional Story* (Quality Words In Print), a joint diary with Robert Winson, *Dirty Laundry: 100 Days In A Zen Monastery* (La Alameda Press, New American Library) and a book on writing, *Unbroken Line: Writing In The Lineage of Poetry* (Sherman Asher Press). Her most recent book of poetry is *Rag Trade* (La Alameda Press). She runs the creative writing program at Santa Fe Community College and is the editor of "Santa Fe Poetry Broadside" (sfpoetry.org).

Kali is an aspect of the great goddess Devi, the most complex and powerful of the goddesses. Kali is one of the fiercer aspects of Devi, but nonetheless as Shiva's consort, she represents female energy. Kali's aspect is destructive and all-pervading, as she represents the power or energy of time. Her four arms represent the four directions of space identified with the complete cycle of time. Kali is beyond time, beyond fear ... her giving hand shows she is the giver of bliss. Because she represents a stage beyond all attachment, she appears fearful to us. So, she has a dual aspect— both destroyer of all that exists and the giver of eternal peace.

This image is from drawings by women of Mithila, India.